Japanese
Street Slang

Japanese Street Slang

Peter Constantine

WEATHERHILL

BOSTON & LONDON

2011

Weatherhill
An imprint of Shambhala Publications, Inc.
Horticultural Hall
300 Massachusetts Avenue
Boston, Massachusetts 02115
www.shambhala.com

9 8 7 6 5 4 3 2

Second Edition
Printed in the United States of America

♾ This edition is printed on acid-free paper that meets the
American National Standards Institute Z39.48 Standard.
♻ This book is printed on 30% postconsumer recycled paper.
For more information
please visit www.shambhala.com.

Distributed in the United States by Random House, Inc., and
in Canada by Random House of Canada Ltd

Designed by Deborah Hodgdon

Library of Congress Cataloging-in-Publication Data
Constantine, Peter
Japanese street slang / Peter Constantine.
     p.   cm.
Romanized Japanese phrases with English translations.
Includes index.
ISBN 978-1-59030-848-6 (pbk.: alk. paper)
1. Japanese language—Slang. I. Title.
PL697.C66 2011
495.6′7—dc22
2010032322

Contents

Foreword

One reason why I have gotten more pleasure and less exasperation from studying Japanese than from studying Chinese is that the dictionaries of Japanese are so much better: when I need information about the meaning, usage, and pronunciation of Japanese words, I can consult works that give me relatively easy access (easy, at least in relation to the obstacles that are posed by what is without doubt the world's screwiest writing system) to detailed and reliable information about the words. And when I use Japanese dictionaries, whether bilingual ones or monolingual dictionaries such as an educated Japanese would use as a reference work on his native language, I am usually rewarded with a kind of pleasure that I often experience in Japan or when dealing with mechanical or intellectual products that emanate from Japan: the joy of appreciating master craftsmanship and of feeling vicariously the pride that the craftsman takes in a job well done. Chinese chefs have often given me that type of pleasure (which enhances the purely sensory pleasure given by the products of their kitchens), but Chinese lexicographers have not.

However, despite the extraordinarily high standards that have been observed in Japanese lexicography, perhaps the highest standards that are maintained for dictionaries of any language, there are major gaps in the standard dictionaries of Japanese, and Peter Constantine's *Japanese Street Slang* fills many of these gaps. Japanese dictionary makers have given no more than sporadic coverage to the numerous words that are generally regarded as impolite or vulgar, and have thereby helped to foster the widely held misconception that Japanese is deficient in those important areas of vocabulary. *Japanese Street Slang* will leave no doubt in any reader's mind that Japanese is as rich as any European language in words that refer raunchily to all known forms of sexual activity, that refer contemptuously to mental, moral, anatomical, and physiological shortcomings of other persons, or that make light of conditions ranging from flatulence and bad breath to pregnancy and poverty.

Standard dictionaries likewise give little if any coverage to vocabulary that is the property of particular occupational groups, social milieus, and other segments of Japanese society rather than of the society as a whole. True, there is extensive coverage of the technical vocabularies of science, engineering, medicine, and biology, but those vocabularies are still conceived of as belonging to Japanese society as a whole, unlike the words that doctors use when talking informally with other doctors, or computer nerds when talking informally with other computer nerds, which do not make it into the dictionaries and remain in the mouths, ears, and minds of the members of those specific subcultures. *Japanese Street Slang* provides a wealth of information about the vocabularies of several subcultures that are far from the center of polite Japanese society: not only the worlds of prostitutes, gays and lesbians, drug users, and thieves, but also that of teenagers, whose vocabulary changes as rapidly as does that of their American counterparts and is also about as opaque to their elders. The difference between the vocabularies that are in the dictionaries and those that are not is like the difference between *vous* and *tu* in French: if you're not a dentist, you can use words like "incisor" and "premolar" to refer to teeth, but you'd better not ask your dentist to "check for caries upper left four, mesio-buccal," since only those who are entitled to say *tu* to the field of dentistry are entitled to use that kind of language. When the author of *Japanese Street Slang* tells his

readers to be very careful about using the words that he introduces them to, his message isn't so much that you shouldn't
say *fuck* to your Aunt Hilda as that you shouldn't say *tu* to subcultures that you're only entitled to say *vous* to, and it may be
useful to think of his warnings in those terms: before you refer
to opium as *kuro,* think about whether you want to affect the
role of an insider to the world of drug-dealing.

    Japanese Street Slang is a delightful book in which to
browse—each example could be a line in the middle of a very
entertaining movie, and one can hardly help imagining those
nonexistent movies as one reads. It provides enough amuse-
ment to be an excellent Christmas present for one's friends
(though probably not for one's parents). But it is also so phe-
nomenally rich a source of information about the Japanese language that is otherwise inaccessible to *gaijin* (the most common
Japanese term for occidentals—I like to translate it as "long-
nosed, round-eyed, hairy barbarian") that it should be on the
bookshelves of any serious translator of modern Japanese fiction and of any library that has even a small collection of books
on the Japanese language.

    Much of both the value and the fun of *Japanese Street Slang*
comes from Constantine's extremely apt English translations,
which reproduce with remarkable accuracy not only the content
of each Japanese example but the connotations of nonchalance,
flippancy, annoyance, anger, or disgust that are apparent in it. It
is a shame that earlier dictionaries did not have on their staffs
a writer / translator with Constantine's formidable skill at con-
veying the "register" of a translated example; perhaps then the
1927 edition of *Kenkyusha's Japanese-English Dictionary* would
have translated *Kuso demo kue* (literally, "Eat shit") not as "A fig
for you" but as the far more accurate "Go fuck yourself." Among
the beneficiaries who will especially profit from *Japanese Street
Slang* are the writers of subtitles for Japanese films, who will

find in Constantine's translations ideal models for many of the lines in gangster movies and low-life comedies that they might otherwise have been hard put to translate.

Constantine informs me that the examples that he presents in *Japanese Street Slang* correspond to only a small part of the copious information that he has gathered about how the members of subcultures at and beyond the fringes of polite Japanese society speak, and how the members of polite society speak when they aren't being so polite. I hope that the growing circle of Japanophile readers will demand that Constantine continue enlightening and entertaining them by sharing more of the contents of his filing cabinet with them in sequels to *Japanese Street Slang,* and by replenishing his filing cabinet through more of the highly productive linguistic field research that made it possible for him to write *Japanese Street Slang.*

James D. McCawley
Professor of Linguistics and of
East Asian Languages and Civilizations
University of Chicago

Introduction

Japanese Street Slang sets out to accomplish two basic tasks: first, to paint a detailed and uncensored panorama of the rich body of forbidden Japanese—the kind of language that no dictionary would dare print; and second, to attempt, by analyzing the more private, jealously guarded secrets of modern Japanese speech, to present more realistic portraits of men and women from different walks of contemporary Japanese life.

When I began writing the first edition of this book in the 1980s, many of my Japanese friends and several scholars expressed concern at what one summed up as "washing our dirty linen in public." The general consensus was that "Foreigners should not learn bad language," often followed by, "And anyway, we don't have any bad language!" The lexicographer and linguist in me rebelled against this unscientific stance. It was proving to be a major hurdle in my initial research. Wherever I turned, I encountered friendly Japanese faces gently declaring: "We do not say such things in Japanese." It was this denial that drove me to hunt through the seediest Japanese establishments, microphone in hand, ready to catch bad words. I was not prepared for what I found.

The biggest obstacle was the sense of privacy that seems to be instinctive in all Japanese. Is it a mechanism used to shield foreigners from contact with *warui kotoba*, "bad words"? If it is, it has duped many a Japanologist into believing that the Japanese language is deficient when it comes to powerful and provocative slang. My initial expectations were summed up by a line in

Jack Seward's *Japanese in Action:* "The Japanese lag behind us Westerners in the sheer beauty, sustained invention, and gasp-producing force of our native insults."

At that point, English slang still seemed to me the richest body of strong and direct language capable of a straightforward frankness unmatched elsewhere.

Wrong!

Once I began digging, I found Japanese street language everywhere. My Japanese friends introduced me to their friends, who in turn introduced me to *their* friends. These people came from all walks of life: high school and university students; show-business people of every shape, size, and description; gamblers and criminal elements—all contributed their shockingly vital and expressive language. My original intention had been merely to investigate insults and swear words, but I was overwhelmed by the richness of Japanese street language.

My research did away with any remaining preconceptions. Time after time, I found Japanese terms that were precise and unambiguous, razor-sharp in their specificity, words that could encompass a whole English phrase, sentence, or even paragraph. For example, English, along with its neighboring Western languages, boasts of thousands of risqué anatomical terms of a sexually explicit nature, but for the most part these are synonyms which, when it comes to actually describing these organs, turn on their puritanical heel and run.

Not so with Japanese. While formal Japanese is formidable at euphemism and understatement, Japanese street lingo is just as formidable in its frankness, abruptness, and uncanny precision.

To present the clearest picture of the capacity and scope of Japanese slang for a new millennium, I decided not to limit myself to everyday slang and colloquialisms used and understood by the general population, but also to pry open the closed doors of Japanese subcultures in order to expose the jealously guarded private languages. When one considers the special properties of Japanese slang, an important national characteristic comes strongly to the fore: while in the West we like to think of ourselves as individualists, cultivating—to use a Japanese neologism—*mii-izumu,* "me-ism," the Japanese prefer to identify themselves with *uii-izumu,* or "we-ism." As Edwin O. Reischauer says in *The Japanese:* "The Japanese are much more likely than Westerners to operate in groups, or at least to see themselves as operating that way. Where Westerners may at least put on a show of independence and individuality, most Japanese will be quite content to conform in dress, conduct, style of life, and even thought to the norms of their group."

Belonging to a group or subculture in Japan means more than dressing alike, thinking alike, and acting alike as a manifestation of psychological commingling. In Japanese street culture, identifying with a group by way of language plays a more important role than it does in subcultures in the West. Students, Tokyo techies, juvenile delinquents, the police, the Yakuza Mafia, different criminal elements, and groups involved in varieties of sexual behavior, all have their individual lingos that border on jargon.

These varieties of slang serve to strengthen the "we-ism" bond of a group, to reinforce solidarity, and to exclude nonmembers, but they also play another important role: they provide the various street elements with specific terminology that the standard language lacks. Words like these, which play such an important role in the complete picture of modern Japanese street slang, are known as *ingo,* or "hidden language." Like a real language, *ingo* is made up of many different dialects—in this case, lingos—nurtured by the different street societies, such as thieves of every persuasion, gangsters, or the sex business (which has its own specific subjargons, such as those used in soapland and "health" massage parlors, "image clubs," prostitution rings, and the like).

The *ingo* segment of street slang in Japan, unlike teen slang and cool urban speech, does not look to the West for linguistic inspiration. While the fashionable club set, the Tokyo crowd, and young urban professionals all over Japan saturate their speech with American, American-inspired, or hybrid Anglo-Japanese expressions, the rougher street elements shun foreign-word imports and absorb the time-honored vocabulary of the crowd they identify with, often using words that sometimes reach back to street speech of the Edo period (1603–1868). Having gathered this hitherto uncollected body of Japanese, ranging from hidden and taboo language to the trendiest new expressions on the scene, I set about my final task as detective-lexicographer, which was to shadow these words that are shunned and denied by standard speech, and to pinpoint their etymological origin.

In the past two decades since I began my research for the initial 1992 edition of this book, spectacular changes have come to the Japanese slang scene. While Yakuza slang or the language of the sex trade has remained surprisingly conservative, other areas of slang have undergone dramatic changes. The young and fashionable cliques, the cyberspace crowd, the computer geeks, the anime aficionados, have all contributed to a vibrant new Japanese street language. In the 2007 TV sitcom *Bubble Fiction: Boom or Bust,* a young Tokyo woman is spiraled back to 1990, to a world without iPhones, modern conveniences, or cyberspace with its many virtual realities. She is utterly disoriented. The world of twenty years ago is as alien to her as the 1990s catchphrases and slang. This sitcom also reflects the fundamental difference between the new 2011 edition of *Japanese Street Slang* and the original book. The young woman in the TV sitcom—a Tokyo bar hostess of the new millennium—would never use expressions like *Ikasu!* (Groovy!) or *Mechanko gū!* (Messed-up good!), nor would she know that the *Shindarera furaito gyaru*—the "Cinderella flight girls"—were moneyed, young professional women of the late 1980s who flew to foreign resorts on weekends in order to have fun with jet-setting men. The extravagances of the eighties are long gone, and the trend-words of the 2010s, with its dire economic crisis, reflect this stark new reality. The *nekafue-nanmin,* "Internet cafe refugees," for instance, are young urban Tokyoites who can no longer afford an apartment and are now living in Internet cafe cubicles, which they can rent cheaply by the day. *Uchigohan,* "home food," is the sullen term for the simple home-cooked meals that have replaced fine dining, while the even more unfortunate *bentoo danshi,* "lunch-box men," are now reduced to bringing lunch boxes from home, as even a stop at the local *Sutābakusu* (Starbucks) is an impossible luxury.

Slang never stands still: new eras bring new words.

The Ins and Outs of Japanese Slang

FOREIGN WORDS

The most prominent general characteristic of modern Japanese slang is its reliance on Western languages, notably English, for inspiration and new words. These terms are known as *gairaigo,* "words from outside," and range from expressions like *adaruto saito* (adult website) and *gei naito* (gay event at a nightclub) to more creative words such as *nō-pan,* short for "no panties" and *ribāshiburu* (reversible), meaning "versatile": a gay or lesbian who can take on either an active or a passive sexual role, depending on the partner's preferences.

The first foreign words to hit Japan were Chinese expressions, which arrived with the first written characters brought by migrant scholars in the fifth century C.E. For centuries these characters and the words associated with them were revered as official and scholarly (much like the higher falutin' words of Latin origin in English).

In the meantime, the first Western influences were making themselves felt. In the 1540s the Portuguese arrived in Kyushu in southern Japan, followed soon after by the Spanish. By the seventeenth century a Portuguese-Japanese pidgin, seasoned with Spanish words, had evolved in the port towns serving the booming trade (which, by the way, specialized in rifles). To this day the Japanese language has preserved words of Portuguese origin like *tempura* (from the Portuguese *tempero,* "flavoring"); *tabako,* "cigarettes" (from *tabaco*); *karuta,* "card games" (from *carta,* "card"). Spanish words in the Japanese language that are still encountered colloquially today are words like the favorite sponge cake of Japan, *kasutera* (from *pan de Castilla,* "Castilian bread"), and *pan,* "bread," from the Spanish word *pan.*

The next torrent of foreign words absorbed by Japanese slang came from Dutch. In 1636 the military government of Japan, the Tokugawa Shogunate, had forbidden all contact with the West, plunging Japan into a virtual isolation that was to last until the Meiji Restoration of 1868. Throughout these two centuries, only the Dutch managed to keep a trading post open, in Nagasaki. The Nagasaki dialect readily picked up many Dutch expressions from the colorful Netherlandic-Japanese pidgin that evolved in the port, and these expressions then found their way into standard speech. Many Dutch words have survived in the Japanese language to this day, like the slangy *otemba,* "romp" or "tomboy" (from the Dutch *ontembaar,* "untamable"), or the now-standard words *biiru,* "beer" (from *bier*), and *garasu,* "glass" (from *glas*).

The big boom came with the Meiji Restoration of 1868, when Japan's doors were flung open to the West. This brought a flash flood of Western words and ideas. Some fanatics were so enthusiastic for all things foreign that there was even a serious movement to abolish the Japanese language altogether. Fascination for the Roman alphabet and its possibilities started the trend in Japanese slang, popular to this day, of using letters as substitutes for words. Some early examples are *U* for *ūman*, a Japanese pronunciation of "woman"; *BA*, pronounced *bi-ei*, for "baba," "old woman"; and *S*, pronounced *esu*, standing in for "singer," meaning in this case "geisha."

The establishment of a strong Japanese navy before the turn of the twentieth century brought another influx of foreign words, especially into the red-light districts of the major Japanese ports. Some of the more granular imports from American and British ports were *go taimu* (go time), the duration of a sexual encounter; *nambā* (number), to experience more than one climax (and by extension, its verb form *nambaru*, to have more than one orgasm); *shōto* (short), a quick sexual experience, as opposed to an all-nighter; *sukuriin* (screen), for the hymen; and *stuan* (stand), for erection.

While red-light-district slang was receiving its first major injection of foreign words, the Meiji in crowd developed its own slang, notoriously fortified with newly acquired English terms. Expressions like *ōrai*, as in "all right," spread like wildfire, even attaching themselves to Japanese words, resulting in expressions like *ōrai geishu*, "all-right geisha"—a geisha whom we would describe today as "an easy lay." Some of the terms adopted from Western languages were exotic even to a Western ear (as is still sometimes the case): a notorious example is the word *kame*, referring to the European lapdog that became the rage in Japan during the Meiji period. (In popular novels of the time, every fashionable heroine had a charming little *kame* or two.) This modish Meiji word is said to have originated when a Japanese overheard a foreigner say "Come here!" to his European doggie.

A contemporary trend of English words in Japanese—particularly in young and fashionable speech—cuts and remixes foreign terms into new attractive word cocktails, often clipping words before fusing them with other words. *Aikora*, for instance, comes from "idol collage" and refers to a doctored photograph of an "idol," where the star's head has been collaged onto a nude body. *Onapetto* is a contraction of "onanie" as in masturbation, and "pet" as in starlet, and refers to a young star or a picture of a star before which one likes masturbating. *Deriherusu* is short for "delivery health spa," and is a new creative euphemism for escort service, where the young hosts or hostesses are sent out to the customer's house to perform house calls.

Today, English words and expressions in Japanese slang come in four guises:

Directly imported from English, keeping their original meaning

> **Wākingu pua.** Working poor.
> **Hōmuresu.** Homeless.
> **Terefuon sekkusu.** Telephone sex.
> **Sentātan** (center tongue). A piercing of the tongue center.

English words or word concoctions, made in Japan, that have taken on new and whimsical meanings

> **Aimasuku** (eye mask). A blindfold used for S-M situations.
> **Anarā** (anal-er). A person who performs anal sex.
> **Andahea** (underhair). Pubic hair.
> **Bakku** (back). Anal sex.
> **Niūhāfu** (new-half). A transgender person.
> **Penisubando** (penis band). A strap-on dildo.
> **Rippusābisu** (lip service). Fellatio offered in a sex-trade establishment.
> **Rongupurei** (long play). The long, expensive session at a massage parlor.

Contractions of two or more English words into a Japanese neologism

> **Arafo** (around forty). Forty-something.
> **Bidebo** (video box). A private porn booth.

Erokēmā (erotic game maniac). A person addicted to pornographic computer games.

Kosupure (costume play). A trend in which people dress up as their favorite anime characters.

Metabo (metabolic syndrome). A fat person.

Rabume (love mail). A love relationship carried out by e-mail and in chat rooms.

Sekuhara. Sexual harassment.

Serebitchi (celebrity bitch). A strong and popular woman.

English words turned into new Japanese verbs

Getto suru (to do "get"). To get.

Masu (to mast). To masturbate.

Rezuru (to lez). To have lesbian sex.

Romu (to roam). To loiter in Internet forums and chat rooms without posting messages.

Dialects

Over the centuries, slang fashions have infiltrated through different dialects. For instance, when Kyoto was Japan's capital (until 1600), the Kansai dialect was dominant and was imitated throughout the nation. The current Japanese idiom began to take shape during the early seventeenth century, when the government was moved to Edo, today's Tokyo. By the end of the eighteenth century, the Tokyo dialect had usurped the Kyoto dialect.

Today's regional dialects, bristling with uniquely local terminology, offer an important source of inspiration for Japanese slang. While the young and trend-conscious generations of the past fifty years throughout Japan looked to Tokyo for linguistic inspiration, smoothing out their dialect speech and imitating the talk of the capital, the new generation of the 2010s is interested in making its speech more fun by using odd dialect words and expressions. There is much fun dialect to be heard on TV, in computer games, in manga comics, and in anime. The *Manga Hōgen Jiten* (manga dialect dictionary) helps these youngsters clarify words used by their favorite comic characters who speak dialect. And there are the *namadoru*, dialect idols who are fashionable, and young entertainers, singers, and young stars who speak in dialect, such as Hikari Okada from Fukui, and Megumi Kusaba from Fukuoka. Fans buy teach-yourself-dialect CDs, and more specifically the CDs produced by these idols, and carefully practice the dialect in question.

Modern Osaka dialect has provided mainstream slang with many words and expressions, like *aho* (fool); *omeko* (vagina); *"Aa shindo!"* (Man, I'm beat!); or *"Mō akimahen!"* (I've had enough!). This trend among younger speakers has been popularized by the mass media, especially comedians and idols from the Osaka area, and has been baptized by Japanese linguists as *shin hōgen*, or "new dialect," of which there are many examples in this book.

The Osakan sentence-ending *nen*, for instance, is very much in vogue. You might hear a young Tokyoite say *"Oishii nen!"* (That's tasty!), or *"Ureshii nen!"* (I'm happy!). Sometimes young Tokyoites slip, mixing standard Japanese and Osaka dialect *"Mō ii nen!"* (Enough already!)—the authentic Osaka form would be *"Mō ē nen!"*

Another popular dialect-ending is *jan. Jan* is a contraction of *ja nai*, which is itself a contraction of *de wa nai*, an informal form of *de wa arimasen*. All of these mean "it is not," or, depending on intonation, the tag "Isn't it?" or "Right?" The slangy *jan* most frequently acts as an emphatic affirmation, as in: *Ii jan!* (Great!); *Kakoii jan!* (Cool, dude!); and *Kimi no kuruma jan?* (It's your car, right?). *Jan* originated in Nagoya and spread into the neighboring dialects of Shizuoka, Yamanashi, and Nagano, and then reached Yokohama, where it became extremely popular in downtown Yokohama slang—so much so that in the following years it became identified nationwide as Yokohamian. *Jan's* final ascent to national stardom began in the late seventies and early eighties, when Tokyoites and other trend-conscious speakers started using *jan* as a send-up of Yokohama speech. By the late eighties and early nineties, *jan* was here to stay.

The other prominent dialect feature that will be encountered throughout the book is the transformation in rough masculine speech of the Japanese diphthongs *ai, oi,* and *ae* into the drawn-out vowel sound *ē*.

> **Shitai** (wanting to do) → **shitē**
> **Sugoi** (super) → **sugē**
> **Omae** (You! or Yo!) → **omē**

Another phenomenon in Tokyo speech is the shortening of words (inspired by neighboring dialects such as Fukushima and Yamagata):

> **Wakaranai!** (I don't understand!) → **Wakannai!**
> **Tsumaranai!** (Boring!) → **Tsumannai!**
> **Shinjirarenai!** (I don't believe it!) → **Shinjinnai!**

The Grammar of Rudeness

Japanese is a language with many levels of diction. For our purposes, we can say that it uses two scales for measuring relations between speakers. The first runs from extreme politeness to extreme rudeness; the second from extreme formality to extreme intimacy. Consider some of the ways of saying "(Someone) is doing (something)," using the verbs *suru*, "to do," and *iru*, which forms the gerund.

> **Shite irasshaimasu.** Honorific.
> **Shite imasu.** Neutral, polite.
> **Shite iru.** Informal; used among friends, often in the contracted form **shite'ru.**
> **Shite-yagaru** or **shi-yagaru.** Offensive.

Suru itself has two additional levels, *nasaru,* which is an honorific form of *suru,* and *yaru,* which is its rude or extremely intimate form.

Finally, an extremely polite form exists in which the honorific *o* is attached to the verb stem, which is followed by *ni naru.*

Nouns as well as verb forms change in response to levels of politeness. The sentence "He / She is reading a book" can serve as an example of all these different levels.

> **Hon o oyomi ni natte irasshaimasu.** Extremely polite and formal.
> **Dokusho o nasatte irasshaimasu.** Very polite and formal.
> **Dokusho o shite irasshaimasu.** Polite and formal.
> **Dokusho o shite imasu. / Hon o yonde imasu.** Neutral and formal.
> **Dokusho o shite iru. / Hon o yonde iru.** Neutral and informal.
> **Hon o yonde-yagaru.** Rude.

Japanese slang usually opts for the ruder and rougher levels of speech.

Pronouns

In talking to others, the choice of pronoun is also important; in fact, the very *use* of a pronoun is a choice in level of politeness, since pronouns are avoided in polite speech whenever possible. To use one at all is to shift your speech toward the informal and intimate.

A special feature of saying "I," "you," "he," "she," or "it" in Japanese is that some pronouns are used exclusively by men (or *very* tough women), and some by women (or men wishing to sound feminine).

I, ME

> **Watakushi.** Formal, polite, respectful. Used by both sexes.
> **Watashi.** Usually feminine.
> **Atashi.** The popular, casual, feminine form in everyday speech.
> **Atai.** Very casual and feminine, used primarily in rough, slangy speech. Its Tokyo-dialect variation *atē* has an even rougher edge to it.
> **Boku.** The masculine equivalent of *atashi,* used in casual conversation by boys and younger men.
> **Ore.** The rougher, tougher, masculine "I," especially favored in slang.
> **Ora.** An even rougher version of *ore.*
> **Washi.** Preferred by older men, it is thought by many to be somewhat unsophisticated and provincial.

YOU

The Japanese pronouns for "you" are often considered too direct and are thus avoided in polite situations. Another option is to use the person's name.

Anata. Formal, and depending upon the context, somewhat feminine. When used by a woman to a man, it can even be translated as "darling," though it is also used between middle-aged men in formal business speech or discourse. The contracted form *anta* is rude and masculine, though tough women use it too.

Kimi. Masculine, casual, and familiar in tone when used among men, and with a rough edge when used by men to women. And a *very* assertive edge when used by women to anyone except children. A female manager, for instance, might use *kimi* to a younger male subordinate.

Omae. Masculine and familiar to the point of roughness. Pronouncing it *omē* makes it even rougher. Very rough women, such as old hands of the sex-trade industry, will also use it.

Temē is rough and too aggressive to use in most situations. *Temē* is especially violent when used to call somebody. It is analogous to the American expression "Yo!" or even "Yo! Asshole!"

HE, SHE

The most respectful reference to a third party in Japanese is *kata* (person) prefaced by *kono* (this); *sono* (that); or *ano* (that, farther away). In everyday conversation, *hito* is substituted for *kata.* These polite and socially safe forms do not appear in the text of this book, as they are rarely used in street slang.

The other two standard words for "he" and "she" are *kare* and *kanojo* (like the English "he" and "she," they can seem rude if used in the presence of the person one is discussing). The Japanese versions of "he" or "she" that one is most likely to meet on the streets of Japan are the abrupt *koitsu, soitsu,* and *aitsu* (stronger than the English "this guy," "that guy," and "that guy there"). They are used only in the most casual circumstances.

IT

Even "it" can be expressed more and less politely. A "thing" is a *mono* in polite, neutral speech, but it becomes a *yatsu* in rougher talk and street slang.

Particles

Standard particles such as *wa, ga,* and *o,* and the question particle *ka,* are often left out in slangy speech (as you will notice in the example sentences throughout the text). Other particles, however, play a very important role in masculine and feminine speech, especially in slang.

FEMININE PARTICLES

No at the end of a sentence in casual speech is generally considered feminine, but nowadays is becoming more unisex.

> *Iku no?*
> You're going?
> *Itsu suru no?*
> When are you going to do it?

    Ne and *nē* as interjections at the end of sentences convey the meaning "Right?" or "Isn't it?" They are generally considered feminine, but are often used by men.

    Wa and the slightly more emphatic *wa yo,* when used as particles at the end of a sentence, are one of the most distinguishing features that mark casual feminine speech.

> *Ii wa.*
> OK.
> *Jodan ju nai wa yo!*
> It's not funny!

MASCULINE PARTICLES

Na and *nā* are generally a rough and masculine sounding version of *ne* and *nē.*

Ze and *zo* are final particles used in rough, masculine, slangy speech. (*Very* few women use them.)

> **Ii zo.**
> OK then.
> **Ore no da ze!**
> This is mine!

In slangy, informal speech, men frequently end their sentences with the copula *da* plus an emphatic *ze* or *zo,* as do assertive women.

A Note on Romanization

In this book, a modified version of the Hepburn system has been used. *N* becomes *m* before *b, p,* and *m.* All long vowels, regardless of their Japanese orthography, are indicated by macrons. An exception is the long *i,* transcribed *ii.*

There is no consensus on the rules for dividing or joining Japanese words. For the purpose of this book, Japanese words resembling prefixes and suffixes, which modify the root term, have been hyphenated to make it easier for the reader to recognize the term being discussed. Prefixes such as *do-, kuso-,* and *chō-,* and suffixes such as *-ppoi, -teki, -kusai, -chikku,* and *-me,* are all examples of these linguistic elements.

Apostrophes play two roles: they indicate contractions, such as *shite'ru* (for *shite iru*) or *itte'n* (for *itte iru'n*); they also mark the semantic and pronunciation distinction between a final *n* and an initial *n* plus vowel, as in *shinin,* "dead person," and *shin'in,* "true cause."

Acknowledgments

All the examples in this book are actual contemporary Japanese slang as it is spoken in different sections of modern Japanese society, from backstreets to school yards, from cyberspace to sex-trade establishments. I overheard some of these examples myself in Japanese bars and clubs, but most came from my many Japanese friends and acquaintances. I am extremely grateful for the invaluable linguistic and cultural information that they provided.

I am most grateful to Ayaka Nishi, who has been a great inspiration and a fountain of knowledge about language and customs, particularly about the young and vibrant talk of the Tokyo streets. I am also grateful to Jonathan Lloyd Goldstein for his insight and perspective on Japanese youth culture, to Erick Paiva Nouchi for his fact-finding missions on Tokyo's nightlife scene, and to Michael Emmerich for his scholarly expertise.

Mark Peterson and I had many discussions over the course of my writing this book, and he has been of great help in finding equivalents in American slang for Japanese expressions.

I would like to express appreciation to Terumi Y., for the endless hours of help and guidance that she offered me in this project. Her long experience in the Tokyo sex trade, and the hours she spent sifting through contemporary Japanese pornography of every kind, did much to illuminate opaque practices in contemporary Japanese society.

I am especially grateful to Wakako I., for checking the Japanese examples and for providing much information on school and university slang. Her deep interest in Japanese inspired me to probe more deeply into the etymology of these slangy and controversial expressions.

I would also like to thank Ryota I., for his help and information in shaping this book. I am especially indebted to him for his frank, open-minded discussions of terms and their usage, and for his help in analyzing modern expressions of dialect origin; Yoko K., for the information on the language used by today's more mature street criminals; Kazu and Taka, for their information on the Japanese drug trade and its language; Naoko, for her invaluable help in identifying words of Osaka, Kyoto, and Nagasaki extraction, and for her help with teenage slang; Yukio, who thanks to his extensive involvement in the Tokyo and Osaka bar scene, was able to supply me with many intriguing anecdotes and expressions; and Christine H., a Westerner who was born, raised, and educated in Japan in a Japanese family, for her many interesting and objective observations on all things Japanese.

I am especially grateful to the late Professor James D. McCawley for his invaluable help and advice. I would also like to express my thanks to Raphael Pallais for his enthusiastic support, and to Mark Peterson for his help with American slang. I am also very grateful to the staff of the Oriental Division of the New York Public Library for their friendly scholarly assistance.

Finally, I'd like to thank all my friends at Meiji University who stalked the streets of Tokyo on the lookout for new ear-catching street slang.

A Warning

Many of the Japanese expressions featured in this book are extremely potent.

Beware of using them inadvertently.

(AI. Love.)

Ai is not a word to be taken lightly. It corresponds to the luminous Greek term "agape," spiritual love, as opposed to "eros," sexual love, which is *koi* in Japanese.

The word *ai* was imported from China by way of Korea during the Asuka period (538–710) by migrant Chinese and Koreans who brought with them the first written characters to Japan. (The same character is used in Chinese, pronounced *ai* in Mandarin; in Korean, it is pronounced *ae*).

Ancient and distinguished as *ai* is, it turns up in all walks of Japanese life, especially in its verb form *ai suru*, "to love."

> ***Ai shite'ru yo!***
> I love you!
> ***Anta dareka ni koi shite'n no? Kao ni kaite aru yo!***
> You're in love with someone, right? It's written all over your face!

A cautious Japanese will try to avoid *ai* if possible, as the very force that renders it so compelling can backfire, making the speaker sound too pushy or too desperate. So for safer, casual conversations about love, *suki*, "like," and *daisuki*, "really like," often prove to be more prudent choices.

> **Daisuki da yo!**
> I like you a lot!
> **Anta atashi no koto suki ja nai'n deshō! Tada atashi to netai'n deshō!**
> You don't love me! All you wanna do is sleep with me!

The two standard Japanese words for lover are *aijin* and *koibito*, both meaning "love person." Of these, *aijin* is the more potent expression, referring to the person that a married man or woman is having an illicit affair with. *Koibito*, on the other hand, is a unisex word for boyfriend or girlfriend.

> **Aitsu no nyōbo Yokohama ni aijin ga iru rashii ze.**
> It seems his wife's got a lover in Yokohama.
> **Anata no koibito dare?**
> Who's your boyfriend?
> **Koibito boshuchū.**
> I'm looking for a lover.

In everyday Japanese, one specifies boyfriends and girlfriends by turning the personal pronouns *kare*, "he," and *kanojo*, "she," into nouns: *watashi no kare*, "my boyfriend" (literally, "my he"), and *boku no kanojo*, "my girlfriend" (literally, "my she"). In more casual speech, *kareshi* (Mr. He) is the preferred word for boyfriend.

> **Nē! Anta ima no kareshi to kekkon suru no?**
> So, are you gonna get married to the boyfriend you have now?
> **Ore no kanojo 'tte beddo de sugēn da ze! Omē ni misete yaritē yo na!**
> Man, my girlfriend's hot in bed! You should see her!

Another slang term favored in casual conversation is *kore*, "this," an expression invariably accompanied by a hand movement designating the sex of the lover in question: a fist with a raised thumb (the nail facing away from the speaker) indicates a male lover, while a fist with a raised little finger (the nail facing the speaker) indicates a female lover.

> **Atashi kanojo no kore kinō michatta.**
> I saw her boyfriend yesterday.
> **Omē kon'ya omē no kore to dekake'n no ka?**
> You going out with your girl tonight?

Two foreign imports that have become as common with younger speakers as *kareshi* and *kanojo* are the English-derived *bōifurendo*, "boyfriend," and *gārufurendo*, "girlfriend."

> **Eee!? Anta no bōifurendo nijūgo! Chotto toshi ja nai?**
> Your boyfriend's twenty-five? That's a bit old!
> **Ore no gārufurendo tsumannē! Okimari no sekkusu shika dekinē!**
> My girlfriend's so boring! All she's into is regular sex!

New words that reflect a more fast-paced lifestyle are *imakare* (now he), the boyfriend of the moment, and *imakano* (now she), the girlfriend of the moment. *Maekare* (before he) is a past male lover, and *maekano* (before she), a past female lover. Someone who is a "friend with benefits" but not an all-out lover, is a *sekufure* (a contraction of "sex friend"), or *esu-efu*, the initials SF.

As distinctions between real and virtual love blur, there are new types of relationships with words to pinpoint them. The *riakare*, a contraction of *riaru* (real) and *kare* (boyfriend), is the boyfriend one meets in real life, as opposed to an online boyfriend, and *riakano*, a contraction of *riaru* and *kanojo* (girlfriend), is the real-life girlfriend. But many relationships are now termed as *rabume* (love mail)—as in love-by-e-mail—or the suggestive but innocent *yubikoi*, "finger love," which refers to love relationships conducted by text message (that is, thumbs pressing the keypad of a cell phone). *Chakare* is the "chat boyfriend" with whom one interacts intimately in chat rooms, and *chakano* is the "chat girlfriend." For the millions of Japanese aficionados of the *hangame* Korean game portal, virtual boy-friends and girlfriends are called *hankare* (*han* boyfriend) and *hankano* (*han* girlfriend).

When an online or off-line lover is no longer of interest, young slangsters use the English-Japanese hybrid phrase *auto obu ganchū,* "out of the running."

(ASOKO. The sexual organs.)

Asoko, "over there," is Japan's number one expression, used by old and young, to refer to male or female private parts. *Kanojo no asoko,* "her over there," can mean "her vagina," "her clitoris," or the whole sexual organ, while *kare no asoko,* "his over there," might refer to "penis," "testicles," or both.

> **Nureta asoko.**
> A wet pussy.
> **Aitsu no asoko ga chiisai / ōkii.**
> His thing's small / large.
> **Aitsu no bikini wa pichipichi dakara, asoko ga mieru.**
> Her bikini's so small you can see her thing.
> **Boku no asoko ga gin gin tatchatta.**
> My thing got rock hard.

Another important word to know is *mono,* "thing." While *asoko,* "over there," is used for all sexual organs, *mono* is lim-ited to the male genitalia because it carries the connotation of a tangible, solid object.

> **Oi! Ore Ken no mono shawā de michimatta yo! Kyōdai!**
> Man! I saw Ken's thing in the shower! It was humongous!

> **Atashi ima made kare no mono mita koto nakatta yo.**
> I still haven't seen his thing.

Another roundabout reference to the male sexual organ is *are*, "that." (People shy away from using *are* to refer to the female organ because it is also a popular synonym for a woman's period.)

> **Kanojo ga iru dake de, ore no are kataku naru'n da yo na.**
> When she's in the room, my thing gets hard.
> **Anta no are iren'no? Tetsudatte ageru wa.**
> Can't you get your dick in? I'll help you.

(BAKA. Idiot.)

This is the most popular Japanese insult. Everyone and everything can be, look, or sound *baka*. In Tokyo the word has lost much of its punch, as "damn" or "shit" have in America. Outside Tokyo, however, it often still carries its pristine meaning, so be careful, especially in Osaka, where it really means "imbecile" or "mentally deficient."

> ***Baka da!***
> He's an idiot! (or That's stupid!)
> ***Baka jan!***
> What an idiot!
> ***Baka yarō!***
> Stupid idiot!
> ***Baka mitai!***
> That's stupid!

Over the centuries, *baka* has been written with many different characters. One of the more entertaining compounds uses the two characters *ba*, "horse," and *ka*, "deer," legend having it that a foolish king of the ancient Chinese Qin dynasty, upon seeing a deer, fatuously said *ba* instead of *ka*, and thus was the first to have earned himself the sobriquet *baka*. Its first appearance in writing was during the fourteenth century, in the tales of the *Taiheiki*, but some scholars have traced it back to ancient Heian words like *waka* and *wakawakashii* (pronounced today *bakabakashii*, "idiotic"), both meaning "infantile," or "simpleminded."

> ***Baka yamerō yo!***
> Don't be such an idiot!
> ***Baka yatte'n ja nē yo!***
> Cut the crap!
> ***Baka itte'n na yo!***
> Don't talk shit!
> ***Baka na koto iu na yo!***
> Don't say stupid things!
> ***Sonna koto baka demo chon demo dekiru!***
> Any idiot can do this!*

Other derivatives of *baka* are *bakachin*, *bakamono*, and *bakachon*, all meaning "stupid guy." (*Bakachon* is now generally avoided, as many people think it means *baka*, "stupid," and *chon*, "Korean.")

The word *Ō*, "big," can be added as an intensifier—*ōbakachin*, *ōbakamono*.

> ***Nan da ano bakachin no chūsha no shikata!! Doko de menkyo nusunde kita'n da?***
> Look how this moron parked his car!! Where did he steal his driver's license?
> ***Ano ōbakachin shinkansen de nekonjimatte, okitara mō Ōsaka made itteta'n da yo.***
> That idiot fell asleep in the bullet train and woke up in Osaka.
> ***Omē tada no bakamono da! Damare!***
> You're such an idiot! Just shut up!

---

*This older slang statement is usually avoided because it is erroneously thought to be a racial slur against ethnic Koreans who have been living for generations in Japan, as *chon* is also a derogatory word for Korean. The *chon* is the sound of two sticks banging together at the end of a theater production.

> *Atashi aitsu no pātii ni ittara sā, ano ōbakamono sono*
> *hen no minna ni denwabango oshieten no.*
> I went with him to the party, and the asshole kept handing
> out his number to all the girls there.

Some of the favorite terms for idiot in current Japanese slang
began as provincial expressions originally introduced into mainstream speech as vigorous new insults. The favorite among these
is *aho*, which originated in Osaka but now ranks among the leading
imputations of idiocy in Japanese. *Aho*, analogous to the American
"moron," is often employed in Tokyo slang using (or trying to use)
Osaka syntax: *"Omae aho ya de!"* (Man, you're a moron!)

> *Sekkusu no tochū de onara o suru nante, omae aho da na!*
> You mean you farted while you were having sex! Man,
> you're a real moron!
> *Omē mata kuruma no kagi nakushita 'tte! Kono aho!!*
> You idiot! You lost your car keys again!!
> *Ano aho! Kinō gohai mo denwa shite kite yagan'no!*
> *Jōdan ja nai wa yo!*
> That butthead! He called me five times yesterday!

Another Osaka term for idiocy heard throughout Japan
is the melodious *ahondara*, a combination of *aho*, "idiot," and
-dara, an emphatic Kansai-dialect suffix. An *ahondara* is a slow
witted imbecile. It has an oldish ring to it, somewhat like "klutz"
or "kook" in American English, but has been picked up by the
young crowd, often appearing in their slang as the acronym
AHDR, pronounced *eieichidiiaru*.

> *Ahondara ya de!*
> What an idiot!
> *Mō atashi ame no naka sanjikan matte'ta no yo! Kono*
> *ahondara!*
> You idiot! I waited for you for three hours in the rain!

> *Tenki no ii hi ni kasa o sasu nante eieichidiiaru ya na!*
> Taking your umbrella with you on a beautiful day like
> this—what a klutz!

Another timeworn insult heard on the streets is *tawake*,
originally imported from the Nagoya dialect. It was created
from the verb *tawakeru*, "romping around." In Nagoyan it was
used of brash and brazen individuals. Its modern meaning has
expanded to include idiots of all kinds.

> *Shinjirarenē! Ano kuso-tawake-me machigatta jūsho*
> *yokoshiyagatta!*
> I can't believe it! That fucking idiot gave me the wrong
> fucking address!
> *Kono kurasu tawake bakkari da! Saitei da yo!*
> This class is fulla boneheads! It's disgusting!
> *Atashi Ken nanka suteta yo! Anna baka na tawake nan*
> *da mon!*
> I dumped Ken! He's such a stupid idiot!

Another provincial insult is *nōtarin*, made up of *nō*, "brain,"
and *tarinai*, "lacking." It was a feature of many dialects—
Ashikaga, Tochigi, Oyama, and Kanuma—before it was picked
up by the older street crowd in the 1970s, and then more recently by the *otaku* (obsessive manga and anime geeks).

> *Ano nōtarin dete itte kurenai ka na! Atashi tsukarete'n*
> *no yo ne!*
> I wish that airhead would leave! I'm tired!
> *Uchi no otōto honto ni nōtarin da yo! Nanimo wakatte 'nai!*
> My brother's such an airhead! He's totally spaced-out!

Another popular insult for weak brains is *usunoro*, a
term that originated at the beginning of the Taisho period
(1912–26) as a conflation of the words *usui*, "weak," and *no-
roi*, "slow."

> *Ano usunoro mata chikoku! Michi machigaetta'n da 'tte yo!*
> That lamebrain was late again! Can you believe he got lost?
> *Aitsu ga mata shiken ni ochita 'tte atarimae da yo!*
> *Usunoro dakara!*
> I'm not surprised he failed his exams again! He's such a
> lamebrain!

Another out-of-town hit, now unfortunately past its prime but still often heard in hard-core street circles, is *otankonasu*, which first appeared in the Utsunomiya, Ashikaga, Sanno, and Tochigi dialects.

> *Ore anna Shibuya kara kita yō na otankonasu-me to*
> *shōbai nanka shinē ze!*
> I don't want any dealings with that jerk from Shibuya!
> *Ore sonna kingaku de sono otankonasu shinyō shinē ze!*
> *Senshū no ikken oboete'ru darō ga!*
> I wouldn't trust that jerk with that kinda money! Remember what happened last week!

Two of the less suave expressions popular today on the Japanese street are *shirinuke* and the somewhat stronger *ketsunuke*, both meaning "ass-less." Both were imported from the Ōtawara and the Utsunomiya dialects.

> *Dete ike! Kono shirinuke-me!*
> Get outta here! You fuckin' jerk!
> *Nani? Atashi anna shirinuke to dēto suru wake nai deshō.*
> What do you mean? Of course I wouldn't go on a date with such a jerk.
> *Pāti ni ita ano onna dare? Nanka ketsunuke jan!*
> Who was that woman at the party? What a total jerk!
> *Atashi takushi de kaetta yo. Datte, ano ketsunuke jibun*
> *no kuruma doko ni tometa ka wasurete'n da mon.*
> I came home by cab, 'cause that asshole couldn't remember where he'd parked the car.

The most recent words for fool and idiot are acronyms in the Latin alphabet from the new *KY-go* (*KY*-slang) that has blossomed in the first decade of the new millennium, used by young people when talking among friends, text messaging, and using Internet chat rooms. The expressions are comical, short, fun—and often quite hurtful.

> **AA (Aho na Anchan).** (My) stupid brother.
> **AB (Anta Baka?).** You stupid?
> **ABK (Aho, Baka, Kasu).** Idiot, fool, scum.
> **ABM (Aho, Baka, Manuke).** Fool, idiot, dunce.
> **ABS (Aho, Baka, Shine!).** Fool, idiot, die!
> **AKT (Aho, Kettobasu!).** Idiot, I'll kick you high into the air!
> **BAS (Baka Aite ni Suruna).** Don't worry about that idiot.
> **BIJ (Baka itten ja nē yo!).** Cut the crap!
> **BKB (Bakabakashii).** Ludicrous.
> **BKNN (Baka Nakuna!).** Stop crying, you idiot!
> **BM (Baka Marudashi).** A fool for all to see.
> **CIA (Chotto Ikareta Aho).** A bit of a crazy fool.
> **DBD (Datte Baka Da Mono).** What do you expect? She / he is an idiot!
> **KAD! (Kono Ahondara!).** What a klutz!
> **OBK (Ōbaka).** A big fool.
> **SBK (Sonna Baka Na!).** That's stupid, no way! or Such a fool!

(BUSU. Ugly.)

This is the worst insult that can be hurled at a Japanese girl, and is most potent when hissed as a drawn-out, sibilant *mmbusss!!* The etymology is a much-debated mystery among Japanese scholars. Some suggest that *busu* was a poison derived from aconite root. A person ingesting the poison would die with a face grotesquely contorted in agony; hence the association. Others suggest that *busu* might be a direct borrowing from the indigenous Ainu language of northern Japan, from *pushu,* meaning "ugly."

> **Nan da kono busu!**
> What a dog!
> **Busu dakedo, ii hito.**
> She might look like shit, but she's a good person.

Hakike ga suru hodo, or *ōēē suru hodo* (enough to make you vomit) can be used to add spice to *busu.*

> **Suzuko wa doressu ga niatte nakute de hakike ga suru hodo busu datta!**
> Suzuko looked so bad in that dress that I almost barfed!
> **Aitsu no kanojo hakike ga suru hodo busu da ze!**
> His girlfriend's ugly as sin!
> **Nani sono kamigata! Ōēē suru hodo busu da yo!**
> What's with that hairstyle? You look like shit!
> **Ore anna ōēē suru hodo busu na onna to dēto shinē yo.**
> I'd never go out with such an ugly troll.

The trend of using alphabet codes in talk among friends and in online chats and text messaging, also includes variants on *busu.* The basic acronym for ugly is *BS* (*busu*), but there are also more intense letter combinations: *HB,* for instance, is short for *honto ni busu* (truly ugly); *TB* for *totemo busu* (totally ugly); and *CBD* for *chibi, busu, debu* (short, fat, and ugly).

> **Atashiku kimpatsu ni sometara, kare ga biiesu (BS) da'tte yū no. Hidoi deshō!**
> He said I looked plug-ugly because I dyed my hair blond. What a bastard!
> **Shinjirareru? Ano eichibii (HB) moderu ni narō to shite'run da yo. Gēē!**
> D'you believe this? That troll wants to become a model. Yeah right!

> *Nan da kono kurabu? Tiibii (TB) darake ja nē ka! Deyō ze!*
> What's with this club? It's full of the ugliest freaks! Let's get outta here!
> *Anna ni akuse tsukemakutta'tte, shiibiidii (CBD) ni wa kawari ga nai yo.*
> Even if she heaps on the jewelry, she's still short, fat, and ugly.

Some more letter combinations:

> **BBC (bibishii)**, for **Busu to Busu no Kyappuru**. An ugly-plus-ugly couple.
> **BK (bikei)** for **Busakimo**. Ugly and creepy.
> **BOK (biiokei)** for **Busu demo OK**. I'm OK with ugly.
> **BSD (biiesudi)** for **Busu Dōshi**. An ugly couple / ugly friends.
> **WBS? (daburuyū biiesu)** for **Watashi'tte busu?** Am I ugly?

Handsome young men are called *ikemen*, a neologism that has become popular in the first decade of the new millennium. (*Ike* is "awesome," and *men* is "face.") Even handsomer than the *ikemen* is the *kamimen* (from *kami*, "god," and *men*, "face"). The unkind neologism for the ugly boy, however, is *busamen*.

(BŪ!)

This is a feisty form of negation, inspired by the loud buzz signal used in popular Japanese TV game shows when the poor contestant chooses the wrong answer.

> *Anta nampa shita?*
> Did you get lucky?
> *Bū!*
> (Thumbs down)

> **Kono natsu Nyū Yōku ni iku?**
> Are you going to New York this summer?
> **Bū!**
> (Thumbs down)

> **Kanojo beddo de yokatta?**
> She good in bed?
> **Bū!**
> (Thumbs down)

The opposite of *bū* is *pinpon* (usually pronounced chirpily as *pin-pōōn*). This comes from the merry cornucopian gong that heralds victory in the TV game-show world.

> **Kinō yatta?**
> Did you get laid yesterday?
> **Pinpōōn!**
> (Thumbs up)

> **Are anta no kuruma ja nai?**
> Isn't that your car?
> **Pinpōōn!**
> (Thumbs up)

> **Miho omae no kanojo?**
> Miho's your girlfriend?
> **Pinpōōn!**
> (Thumbs up)

(CHIRAMISE. Sneak peek.)

Chiramise literally means "glance showing": people intentionally or unintentionally flashing intimate apparel or an otherwise concealed part of the body. Throughout the world, flashing and being flashed has many aficionados, but Japanese *chiramise* has such widespread appeal that it has gained its own "ism" ending: *chiramism* (*chiramizumu*).

People wishing to offer intentional glimpses of underwear will buy specific garments such as a *chiramise T-bakku*, "a flashable thong," *chiramise jii-sutoringu*, "a flashable G-string," and for men, *buriifu chiramise*, "flashable briefs," with eye-catching patterns and colorful waistbands that can peek out above low cut jeans. As the packaging often emphasizes: *Chiramise demo Okei*, "suitable for flashing."

But often the flashing is inadvertent. *Kazechira*, "wind flash," is when the wind blows a skirt up, a situation also known in peeking circles as *sukātomekuri* (skirt flip), and its Japanglish synonym *sukāto rifuto*, "skirt lift." The result is *panchira*, "panty flash," *pan* being short for the English "panties." In rarer cases, when the woman is not wearing panties, the term is *manchira*, "pussy flash," also called *hidachira* and the rougher *mekochira*, which are usually encountered only in pornography or in rough male talk.

In a movie, when an actor or actress flashes an undergarment or body part, the term is *chirashiin,* "a flash scene," and a photographic still is called *chirashotto,* "flash shot," or *mokkorishoto,* "bulge shot," if the still has caught a male bulge.

Using cell-phone cameras, the *nozokima* (peep devil) will discreetly take sneak-peek shots or footage, called *appusukāto,* from the English "up skirt."

Other terms for flashing underwear or parts of the anatomy are:

> **Anachira** (hole peek). Furtive glimpses of anuses, but also vaginas.
>
> **Burachira** (bra peek). A bra peeking out from an unbuttoned shirt or blouse. In cases when a bra shows through a thin fabric, the term is *burasuke* (bra show-through), shortened in slangy speech or excited text messages to its initials *BS*.
>
> **Burichira** (briefs peek). Keeping an eye out for men's briefs became a growing trend after the Japan Professional Soccer League was set up in 1993. The trend spilled over into comics, where handsome male characters give inadvertent between-the-legs glimpses of their underwear.
>
> **Chikuchira**, short for *chikubichira* (nipple peek), is either a nipple that inadvertently slips out of a blouse, or the outline of a nipple that can be seen through the fabric. As showing the outline of a nipple is considered trendy, women who want to wear bras but still give the impression that their nipples are visible can attach to their bras *tsukechikubi* (affixed nipples), also known as *nippuruzu,* the Japanese pronunciation of the English word "nipples." Wearing the garment that allows nipples to stand out is called *munepochi* (breast chubby); *nōbura munepochi* (no-bra breast chubby) specifies a definitely braless showing.
>
> **Chinpoji**, a contraction of *chin* (penis) and *pojishon* (position), is the position of a penis visible through underwear or outer clothing.
>
> **Harachira**. Belly peek.

Harasujichira. Abs peek.

Heachira (hair peek). Pubic hair, sometimes also seen with low-rise jeans. This is also known as *andaheachira* (underhair peek).

Hesochira. Navel peek.

Koshichira. Usually "lower-back peek," but also "hip peek."

Kurichira (clitoris peek). Also known as *mamechira*, "bean peek."

Mekosuji (cunt line). Also its synonym *mankosuji*. The clearly visible line of a vagina when a woman wears tight shorts of thin fabric or lycra, known in American slang as "cameltoe."

Momochira. Thigh peek.

Paichira. Short for *oppaichira*, "breast flash." Also *munechira*.

Penisuchira (penis peek). Also known as *saochira*, "rod peek," and *marachira*, "cock peek." When the full penis is exposed, the term *furuchin* is also used—from *furu*, a combination of the English "full," and *chimpo*, "dick." A rougher term for penile exposure is *namachinko*, "raw dick," a term also used in the sex trade for an uncondomed member.

Tamachira (ball peek). Also known as *kinchira*, short for *kintamachira*, "testicle peek"; *fukurochira*, "sack peek"; and *fugurichira*, "scrotal peek."

Yokochichi (side breast). When a partial or a whole breast is visible from the side of a T-shirt or blouse.

Yokochin (side penis). When the penis inadvertently slips out of the bottom of loose shorts, briefs, or swimming trunks. This is also known as *hamichin*, "jutting penis." When a testicle slips out from under the shorts, the term is *hamikin*, "jutting gold"—*kin* being short for *kintama*, "gold balls" or "testicles."

(CHIKAN. Pervert.)

In crowded places such as Tokyo subways during rush hour, there often lurks a *chikan*, a pervert who will stealthily touch an unsuspecting victim. This encounter is called *chikan ni au,* "encountering a pervert." *Chikan* is made up of *chi*—the Chinese character for "madness" or "derangement"—and *kan*—suggesting a large, strong man. A typical verbal reaction to being molested is *"Kya! Chikan! Tasukete!"* (Yuck! Pervert! Help!), or simply *"Chikan!"*

> **Ano hito chikan mitai.**
> That guy looks like a perv.
> **Manin no chikatetsu de chikan ni atta no! Kimochi warūūi!**
> This creep, like, grabbed me on the subway! It was gross!
> **Atchi ikanai hō ga ii yo! Chikan darake da yo!**
> I wouldn't go there! It's teeming with perverts!

Image clubs (*imkura*) are sex-trade establishments where customers can act out their fantasies. One of the services offered is called *chikan purei,* "pervert play." In the better clubs there are surprisingly realistic simulations of many different places where one can molest or have sex with a character or persona of one's choice. The paying pervert can, for instance, approach a flight attendant pushing a well-stocked drink cart through the aisles of a perfect replica of a Japan Airlines cabin. *Chikan purei* can take place in make-believe subway cars or executive offices, and some clubs even offer *yagai-opushon,* the "outdoor option," where fantasies can be played out in public spaces. This is also called *yagai purei,* "outdoor play," or *aokan,* "green mischief," with the variant service *yagairoshutsu purei,* "outside exposure play."

The female counterpart of *chikan* who touches or rubs against men in crowded areas is the *onna no chikan,* "woman masher"; *onna no sukebe,* "woman creep"; or *chijo. Chi,* as in *chikan,* means "insane" or "crazed"; *jo* means "woman."

> **Mata ano chijo ore no asoko sawatte kita yo!**
> That nympho touched my thing again!

> *Mata asa ano chijo ni atchatta yo!*
> That nympho approached me again this morning!
> *Maitta nā! Densha de onna no sukebe ni atte sā. Mune suriyosete kita'n da ze.*
> Man, I tell you! This freak woman rubbed her breasts against me in the train.

The *chijo* is also popular in new sex-trade establishments such as the *esute* ("aesthetic" massage parlors) and the *deriherusu* (delivery "health" clubs), in which men can choose to remain passive during sexual service and be molested and humiliated. *Chijo* is also a favorite pornographic genre in which aggressive women "molest" defenseless men, with *rezuchijo*, "lesbian molester," as an extremely popular subgenre. This is also called *gyakuchikan kōsu*, "reverse molester menu."

A broad miscellany of eccentric sexual behavior can be rendered by adding the suffix *-ma* ("devil" or "demon") to words that run the gamut from "pinch" to "razor blade."

> *Ashiname-ma*, "foot-lick demon," is a foot fetishist who enjoys licking feet during sex, or as a substitute for sex.
> *Chēnji-ma*, "change devil," is the ever-dissatisfied sex-trade customer who keeps asking for different hostesses.
> *Chikuri-ma*, "pinch devil," approaches his victims (usually female) and squeezes or pinches their bottoms, legs, arms, or breasts.
> *Gōkan-ma*, "rape-devil," is the rapist, also called by the younger crowd *rēpu-ma*, from the English word "rape." Some sex clubs offer *rēpu-gokko*, "rape play," in which customers can pretend to rape hostesses.
> *Kamisori-ma*, "razor-devil," enjoys making slits in women's clothing, usually in the cramped quarters of the rush-hour subway.
> *Kanchō-ma*, "enema demon," is an individual who likes receiving and in some cases giving what in Japanese fetish circles is called an *ero kanchō*, an "erotic enema."

Kōsatsu-ma, "strangling demon," is a mad strangler, or a person interested in asphyxiation bondage games.
Kutsuname-ma, "shoe-lick devil," is the shoe fetishist, who enjoys licking a partner's shoe, usually in a groveling, submissive stance.
Nozoki-ma, "peeping demon," is a voyeur who uses binoculars or cell-phone cameras to observe people doing things like dressing, bathing, or engaging in sexual intercourse.
Sawari-ma, "touch devil," will usually slip his hand up skirts in crowded areas for a quick fondle.

(CHIKUSHŌ! Beast!)

In a situation where an American would say "Shit!" "Damn!" or "Fuck!," a Japanese would say *Chikushō!* (Beast!). It began as a Buddhist word used to differentiate man from beast, but today *chikushō* is one of the stronger expletives.

> *Chikushō! Saifu o wasurechatta!*
> Fuck! I forgot my wallet!
> *Chikushō! Shippai shichatta!*
> Shit! I made a mistake!
> *Chikushō! Densha ni noriokurechimatta ze!*
> Damn! I missed the train!

In a verbal or physical skirmish, Japanese will often shout *chikushō* at each other, with variations such as *konchikushō*, "this beast"; *baka chikushō*, "idiot beast"; and *kuso chikushō*, "shit beast." *Chikushō onna* is an extremely offensive way of referring to a woman, and *chikushō yarō* to a man. Adding *-me*, a suffix that originally meant "cur" or "slave," to any of these *chikushō* terms makes them even more trenchant.

Another abusive attack—one perhaps surprising to non-Japanese—is the simple question, *Nan da yo?* "What is this?"

(*Da yo* is the casual form of *desu*, "to be.") When said directly to someone in a confrontational manner, the simple *Nan da yo?* has the force of the American "What the fuck!" "What the fuck do you want!" or "Fuck off!" Even more violent is *"Nan da yo, omae!"* "What is it, you!"

Other expletives to be uttered judiciously are:

> **Nani yo!**
> What [the hell]! (A version of *"Nan da yo?"* used only by women or feminine men.)
> **Nan da koitsu!**
> What's with him / her!
> **Nani yatte'n da yo!**
> What are you doing!
> **Nanka monku a'kka?**
> You got a problem?

(CHIMPO. Penis.)

Some say that *chimpo* started out as a respectable Buddhist word, written with the characters *chin* (curious) and *po* (treasure); others say that its ancient etymology comes from *chin* (small) and *boko* (spear). But regardless of its provenance, *chimpo* has given rise to a series of popular words for penis. Its childish variant, *chinchin,* has a playful quality that makes it useful in colloquial speech as one of the few direct ways of saying "penis" that is too cute to be crass. *Chinko* and *chimpoko*—or its inverted form, *pokochin*— are light but rougher variants that should be used judiciously in mixed society. All these words can be softened with the honorific *o-* prefix—*ochinchin, ochinko, ochimpo, ochimpoko.*

> **Chiisai / ōkii chinchin.**
> A small / large pecker.

> **Aitsu wa chimpo o shiko shiko suru.**
> He's wanking his dick.
> **Tatta chinko.**
> A hard dick.
> **Chimpoko no atama.**
> A dickhead.
> **Pokochin marudashi de uro uro!**
> He's wandering around with his dick hanging out!

For years *ochinchin* has been the official elementary-school word for penis. In the 1980s, however, much to everyone's surprise, *chinchin* broke out of its masculine semantic confines when the Saitama Board of Education decreed that it was also the only acceptable term for vagina in elementary school sex-education classes. Unfairly enough, Japanese has no term for vagina of an equivalently euphemistic caliber. Perplexed teachers had been resorting to terms like *opampom,* or dubious words fashionable in the sex trade, like *waremechan* (Little Miss Crack). In the 1990s *mechinchin* (girl pecker) was introduced as a solution, and then widely used.

In down-to-earth circles, the group of *chin* words have many variants. You might hear *dekachin* and *dekachinko* in reference to a large, well-proportioned penis. *Deka* (from *dekai*) means "huge," and is a popular word that was adopted from the Osaka dialect.

> **Aitsu no asoko wa dekachin da na!**
> His thing's like a ramrod!
> **Kare no dekachin dakara, hairu to saikō yo!**
> He's hung like a bull! He drives me crazy when he puts it in!

Dekachin is a large but not necessarily erect penis, as is the even larger *gokubutochin* (big-and-thick penis). *Bikubikuchimpo* (jittery penis) is a throbbing or swelling penis, while *bokkichimpo* (stiff penis) simply means "erect penis." *Umanami* (horselike) means "hung like a horse." *Funyachin* is a flaccid penis that either has difficulty becoming erect or cannot achieve erection. (*Funya-funya* means "limp" or "flabby.") *Chōchin*, "paper lantern," is a penis that is large but always flaccid or floppy. Penises thought to be too small or underpowered are called *arachin*, "flawed penis." Men who are troubled by the fear that their penis is too small, are said to suffer from *arachin shōkōgun*, "flawed-penis syndrome."

Mukechin, "peeled penis," is an uncircumcised penis with the foreskin pulled back. *Yokochin*, "side penis," is a penis that accidentally slips out from under the shorts, as is the *hamichin*, "jutting penis," while *furuchin*, "full penis," is used for a penis that is fully exposed.

> **Ore kono pantsu hairanai ya. Yokochin ni natchau mon.**
> I can't wear these shorts. My dick'll be hanging out.
> **Sonna furuchin no mama de arukimawaranaide yo!**
> Don't walk around with your dick hanging out like that!
> **Hayaku mite! Aitsu hamichin shite'ru!**
> Quick, look! His dick's hanging out!

Penis pictures sent over the Internet as e-mail attachments or mobile-phone snapshots (usually to generate blind dates) are called *chinshame*, literally "penis-picture mail."

A playboy obsessed with sex is called a *yarichin* (sex penis), a neologistic derivative of the older *yariman* (sex cunt).

Chinge (penis hair) is a slang term for a man's pubic hair, and *gyarandō* (also *gyarandū*) is the word for the "treasure trail" or "happy trail" that extends up to and around the navel. While *gyarandō* is considered a sexy term, *harage*, "belly hair," is not.

(CHITSU. Vagina.)

This is the official term for vagina, and ranks with *joseiki* (female sexual organ) in formality. It is favored in anatomical textbooks and medical circles, but is considered by many to be too technical for everyday conversation.

> **Tampon o chitsu ni ireru toki wa rerakusu shinai to hairanai yo.**
> If you don't relax, you won't be able to get that tampon into your vagina.

In Japanese, however, technical terms like *chitsu, joseiki, sōnyū* (insertion), or *anaru sekkusu* (anal sex) are regarded titillating in sex-trade circles. Such technical terms offer the most direct and thus the crudest way of calling a spade a spade.

> **Kanojo no chitsu wa itsumo nurete iru.**
> Her vagina is always wet.
> **Chotto kyō chitsu ga itai no yo ne! Yarisugi kashira!**
> My vagina kinda hurts today! Maybe I got too much action!

Particularly surprising words on the sex-trade scene are *bagina, buagina, uagina,* and *wagina,* all from the English "vagina." *Bagina* arrived in Japan as a medical term, along with *penisu* (penis) and *kuritorisu* (clitoris). These words are often preferred to native equivalents, as their foreignness, it is felt, makes them somehow more indirect. Since the pornographic boom of the 1990s and 2000s, these words have gained a raunchy mystique, and are often found in porn movies and related media. The standard Japanese *chitsu* rarely figures in pornographic DVDs; the *bagina* group of words, on the other hand, are more popular.

Less technical words for vagina favored in sex-trade circles are *akagai*, "ark shell"; *awabi*, "abalone"; and, perhaps rather strangely, *momotarō*, "Peach Taro," a popular folk hero who befriended animals and fought ogres.

> **Akagai o yaru.**
> To do pussy.
> **Awabi o nameru.**
> To eat pussy.
> **Juku juku na momotarō.**
> A juicy snatch.

Meiki, "rare utensil," is a particularly good vagina. *Kitsukitsu*, "tight-tight," is a tight vagina, also known as *kitsuman*, "tight pussy." *Kyoki*, "billowing organ," and *gabaman*, are loose vaginas. (*Gababababa* means "oversize.")

The words for clitoris are the English *kuritorisu* and its shortened form *kuri*, as well as *sane*, "kernel"; *mame*, "bean"; and *maron*, "chestnut."

Inshin is the standard word for labia, but in the sex trade *birabira* (petal-petal) is the more common word.

In cheaper provincial establishments, one hears less elegant words for vagina: *moya moya no seki*, "hairy barrier," and *manjū*, "bean-jam bun," are staples, with variants of *manjū* such as *nikumanjū*, "meat bun," and *kemanjū*, "hairy bean-jam bun," similar to the American expression "hair pie" or "fur pie." *Kuma no kawa*, "bear's fur," is used for especially hairy women.

> **Atashi no manjū oishii wa yo. Ajimete minai?**
> My bean-jam bun tastes good. Wanna try?
> **Ore ga ima hoshii no wa kemanjū da.**
> What I need now is some snatch.
> **Chotto matte'te! Ima nikumanjū aratte kuru kara sa!**
> Wait for me here! I'm just going to wash my twat!

Kono nozokibeya wa moya moya no seki miru made ikura harau'n darō?

How much do we have to pay at this peep show before we get to see some snatch?

T-bakku wa pichipichi dakara, kuma no kawa mieru.

Her T-back is so tiny, you can see her hairy twat.

(DANKON. Penis.)

This word literally means "male root." In the sixties, it gate-crashed the world of literature when the controversial poet Shiraishi Kazuko published a poem titled "Dankon." A sample: *"Dankon wa hibi ni gun gun sodachi!"* (The man root grows larger day by day!). Outside of modern poetry, *dankon* appears both in the sex trade and in pornography.

> *Aitsu no gin gin tatta dankon.*
> His hard, throbbing man root.
> *Atashi dankon wa shaburanai.*
> I don't suck dick.

The characters *dan,* "male," and *kon,* "root," are the Chinese reading (*on yomi*), and can also be pronounced in their native Japanese rendition (*kun yomi*), creating another uncouth word for penis: *otokone.*

> *Anta no kare no otokone don'gurai dekai no?*
> So, how big is your guy's dork?
> *Atashi kagiana kara kare ga otokone ijitte'ru no michatta!*
> When I looked through the keyhole, I saw him playing with his cock!

Other root motifs in Japanese words for penis are: *yōkon*, "bright root"; *chōkon*, "super root," for very large penises; *rakon*, "bare root," for "cut" or circumcised penises; *yōkei*, "male stem"; and *hine daikon*, "shriveled radish," used to describe small, wrinkled penises.

> **Onegai dakara, motto yōkon aratte hoshii na.**
> Could I ask you to wash your "bright root" a little better?
> **Ara! Ima made yatta kimpatsu no otoko minna rakon datta yo!**
> You know, all the foreigners I've done till now had cut dicks!
> **Ano onna ni totte, ichiban miryoku-teki na tokoro ga yōkei yo!**
> All this woman is interested in is dick!
> **Bikkuri shichatta! Ano ō-otoko konna ni chitchai hine daikon motte'n da mon!**
> I was so surprised! Such a humongous guy with such a shriveled little dick!

Other sex-trade and street slang words for penis are:

> **Mara**, a religious term meaning "obstacle to Buddhist practice," is considered a particularly rough term.
> **Musuko.** Son.
> **Nikubo.** Meat stick.
> **Rokei**, "exposed stem," is an uncircumcised penis whose foreskin is so short that it looks circumcised.
> **Sao.** Pole.
> **Shinseihōkei**, "genuinely wrapped stem," is a penis whose head is covered by foreskin even when erect. *Hōhi* is the word for foreskin, which is also simply called *kawa*, "skin."
> **Tansho**, "faulty-small," is a small penis.

A relatively recent newcomer on the scene is the popular *penisu*, "penis." Like other imported anatomical words—*bagina*, "vagina," and *kuritorisu*, "clitoris"—*penisu* is now also extensively heard in everyday speech, and in sex talk and pornography. Some recent DVD best sellers:

> ***Aoyama Penisu Saron: Inbu Senjō*** (Aoyama Penis Salon: Genital Wash).
> ***Penisu o Hoshigaru Hitodzuma*** (Married Women Desiring Penises).
> ***Penisu Hantā: Kyonyū Chijo Karareta Emu-Dansei*** (Penis Hunters: Large-breasted Female Perverts Hunt Down Masochists).

(DASU. To ejaculate.)

The verbs *dasu,* "to send" or "to throw out"; *deru,* "to come out"; and *iku,* "to go," are the three most common verbs for ejaculation, parallel to "coming" in America.

To announce an orgasm, one can either use the verbs in their short dictionary form—*dasu, deru,* or *iku*—or add the suffix *-sō* (literally, "it seems like" or "I'm about to"):

> ***Iku . . . iku!***
> I'm coming . . . I'm coming!
> ***Ikisō da!***
> Wow, I'm about to come!
> ***Itta?***
> You came?
> ***Dcso!***
> I'm coming!
> ***Chikushō! Desō! Desō!***
> Oh shit! I'm coming! I'm coming!
> ***Mō dashita? Saitei!!***
> Oh shit!! You came already?
> ***Anta naka de dasanaide yo?***
> Don't come inside me, OK?

Variations on *dasu* are *sotodashi*, literally "outside sending," meaning to ejaculate outside a vagina or anus, while *nakadashi*, "inside sending," means to ejaculate inside.

A rougher synonym for the above verbs is *buppanasu*, "to totally let go," which is equivalent to "shooting one's wad" or "getting one's rocks off."

> ***Ore kinō buppanashita toki, mō owari ka to omotta!***
> When I shot my wad yesterday, I thought I was gonna die!
> ***Aniki ga buppanashita toki, monosugē oto ga shita kara minna ni kikoechimatta!***
> My brother was making so much noise when he got his rocks off that we all heard him!

When a character ejaculates in one of the many pornographic manga, anime, or comics, the onomatopoetic *dopyu*, or *dopyu-dopyu*, "squirt-squirt" is used. Consequently *dopyu* is also a popular word for ejaculation in slang.

> ***Kessa nikai dopyu shita.***
> This morning I squirted twice.
> ***Nakadashi dopyu shita?***
> You squirted inside her?

Ejaculation as a result of masturbation is called *nuku*—a verb that can both mean "to extract" and "to bring a matter to the end." *Nuku* is often used in sex-trade establishments to refer to a customer ejaculating. The technical-sounding *kōnaihassha*, "ejaculation into the mouth," is another sex-trade term common in establishments such as *herusu*, "health" massage parlors, and *menzu esute*, "men's aesthetic parlors." Equally technical is the *zetsujōhassha*, "on-the-tongue ejaculation," and its slangier synonym *berosha*, "tongue shot," in which a masturbating customer can ejaculate onto the tongue of a *kompanyon*, a professional "companion." Other favorites are *gansha*, "face shot," and *nyūnaishasei*, "between-the-breasts ejaculation."

As the customer's ejaculating usually signifies that the session or *sābisu* (service) is over, ejaculation is also professionally referred to as *fuinishu,* derived from the English word "finish."

(DEBU. Fatso.)

Debu is a slangy taunt for fat people.

> **Nan da kono debu!**
> Get a load of fatso!
> **Sonna ni taberu'n ja nai yo! Debu ni naru zo!**
> Don't eat so much! You'll turn into a pig!

But despite being pejorative, over the last decade *debu* has increasingly gained in nuance, also becoming an expression of admiration when used by people attracted to fuller figures, and also an empowered self-description. *Debunaito* (fatso night), for instance, is an event at a club for overweight people. Other common terms are *debugurūpu* (fatso groups); *debukai* (fatso associations); and *debukōen* (fatso support groups). *Deburogu* (a contraction of *debu* and "blog") are blogs by and for overweight individuals.

But as *debu* is still often considered a slur, its insulting tone can be defused by playful reduplication into the cuter *debu-debu. Debu-debu kun* (young Mr. Fat-Fat) is a nicer way of referring to a fat youth, while *debu-debu chan* (Miss Fat-Fat) is often used for plumper girls.

The verb form of *debu* is *deburu,* to grow fat.

> **Aa, chotto debutte kichatta!**
> Oh no, I've put on weight!
> **Dō shiyō? Mata debutchau!**
> What am I gonna do? I'm putting on the pounds!
> **Aitsu honto ni debutte'ru!**
> Man! He's really fat!

> *Sugoi shokku! Ano ko anna ni debutte'ru kara, dare da ka wakaranakatta.*
> What a shock! I didn't even recognize her, she's got so fat!

"To get fat" is *debutte kuru.*

> *Kenji, omae nanka honto ni debutte kita!*
> Shit, Kenji! You've really blown up!
> *Ano ko daietto shite'run ja nai no? Nande anna ni debutte kuru no?*
> Isn't she supposed to be on a diet? How come she's got fatter?
> *Itsumo okashi bakkari kutte'ru kara, debutte kuru'n da yo.*
> You're gonna turn into a blimp if you keep on stuffing your face with candy.

A more upbeat way of describing weight gain is the verb *ponyoru.* "*Ponyotte kichatta!*" has the nuance of "I've gotten all pudgy!"

If *debu* wavers between being acceptable and derogatory, *debusu,* a contraction of *debu* (fat) and *busu* (ugly), is a slur in no uncertain terms. Another slur is *debuota,* a contraction of *debu* and *otaku,* "nerd."

The younger Tokyo crowd, which likes to pepper its speech with Latin-alphabet acronyms, often uses discreet letter *D*, pronounced *dii,* to refer to those who are fat.

> *Aa, ano dii no namae, nan datta ke?*
> Aah, remind me, what was the fat one's name?

Consequently, when a fat person dates another fat person, the unkind acronym is *DVD—debu versus debu.* An even unkinder set of initials is *DSK*, which stands for *debu de sukebe de kusai*—"fat, a lecher, and stinky." Unkinder still is *CDB*, short for *chibi, debu, busu*—"a dwarf, fat, and ugly." Further initials of the moment, usually to be heard in school yards and in the *otaku* Akihabara geek circles:

> **AD (Arienai Debu).** An impossible fatso (fat beyond belief).
> **DK (Debu Kyappuru).** A fat couple.
> **MD (Mukatsuku Debu).** An irritating fatso.
> **MDD (Megane, Debu, Deppa).** Glasses, fat, overbite.
> **UD (Usotsuki na Debu).** A lying fatso.
> **3B (Toripporu Bii).** Triple B: *Baka* (idiot), *Debu* (fat), *Busu* (ugly).

Another newer slang expression for a fat person is *meta-bo,* a word that comes from *metaborikku shindrōmu* (metabolic syndrome). There is also the lighter but equally cruel *panpan-man* (bread-bread man), inspired by the anime series *Anpanman,* whose main character is a little man with a fat round bun for a head. *Zōashi* (elephant legs) is used for a woman with fat legs, the fat legs referred to as *anakonda* (anacondas), and *bonresu-hamu,* "boneless ham," is specifically used for fat legs in fish-net stockings.

A friendly, though probably equally hurtful, method of nicknaming one's fat friends is by adding *bū* (Japanese for "oink") to their name. If Mariko is overweight, her friends might playfully call her Maribū. Ayaka might become Ayabū, and Taro might become Tarobū.

The only truly positive term for the heftier individual is *motepu,* an expression that has surfaced in the last two or three years. *Motepu* is a person, usually a man, who is on the heavy side, but who is considered attractive. *Moteru* means "to be popular," and *puyo-puyo* means "jellylike" or "fat and wobbly."

Men and women who are partial to heavier individuals are called *debusen,* "fat specialists."

(DEKA. Police.)

Many of the informal references to the police force popular in Japan's streets today originated in the late-nineteenth century as Yakuza jargon. Words for police like *gacha, in'ya, ite, jinkoro, mambo, mappo, pēchan,* or *pēshan* started their careers as secret words in clandestine gangster talk, and have remained a part of the underworld lingo.

> ***Ano gacha ore-tachi tsukamaeyō to shita kedo, umaku bakureta ze.***
> That badge tried to nail us, but we managed to get away.
> ***Ki o tsuketa hō ga ii ze! In'ya nanka kagi tsukete'ru ze!***
> We'd better watch it, man! The boys in blue are onto us!
> ***Kono hen no ite yarō, tondemonē kuso-domo da!***
> The fuckin' cops in this neighborhood are real assholes!
> ***Shizuka ni shiro! Mambo ga iru!***
> Quiet! The law!
> ***Konna ni pēshan uro uro shite'tara, ore biku biku shichi-mau yo!***
> I always get nervous when the fuzz are around!

"*Mappo!*" or "*Deka!*" as a warning once had the secretive quality that "Cops!" did when it was first used. The cover of some of these words was blown in Japan when gangster movies became the craze in the 1950s and 1960s. In America as in Japan, word formulas (like "spill the beans" or "hit man") that had been the exclusive property of hardened criminals were suddenly introduced into middle-class homes, cataclysmically expanding the average person's view of the world.

> ***Deka ni kakawaru'n ja nē zo! Ki o tsukero!***
> Careful, man! Don't mess with the cops!
> ***Ano mappo-me nani sama da to omotte yagaru'n da!***
> Who the fuck does that cop think he is!

(EMU. M.)

The initial *M* can have various allusions in Japanese slang. *Emu*, for instance, can represent *musuko*, which means "son," and by extension is frequently used in street slang to refer to the penis.

> ***Aitsu no emu chiisai'n da yo ne!***
> His dick's real small!

Emu is also used as an abbreviation for *masu*, which is itself an abbreviation of *masutabēshon*, "masturbation."

> ***Emu shite'ru!***
> He's jerking off!
> ***Hazukashikatta! Aitsu emu shite'ru toki ni, boku heya ni***
> ***haitchatta kara!***
> Man, I was so embarrassed! When I entered the room he was beating his meat!

In S-M circles, *M* means "masochist," and it appears in various combinations:

> ***Emu purei***, "masochist play," is a sex-club service in which men are humiliated by dominant hostesses. This is also called *emu sābisu*, "M service."

> ***Emudeai*** (M rendezvous). A masochist get-together.
> ***Emu-jo.*** Masochist woman.
> ***Emu-o.*** Masochist man.
> ***Esu-emu kurabu.*** S-M club.

In the new millennium, other areas of Japanese slang have appropriated the letter *M*. Some examples are:

> ***Emu-gō*** (M number). Police jargon for missing person, *M* being short for *misuingu*, "missing."
> ***Emu-ji kaikyaku*** (M-letter legs apart). A masturbatory position in which the person is lying on his or her back with legs pulled up, forming the letter "M."
> ***Emu-tii-efu*** (MtF). A male-to-female transvestite or transgendered person.
> ***Emu-tii-efu-bian*** (MtF-bian). A male-to-female transvestite or transgendered person, who, as a woman, identifies herself as a *bian*, "lesbian."

Another phenomenon of the new millennium has been the increased use of Latin letters as acronyms, both in the speech of teenagers and twenty-somethings and in online chats and text messaging. Some examples of the different meanings that the letter *M* has taken on are:

> ***MG.*** *"Mail-address" o "get" suru,* literally "Get his e-mail address."
> ***MIW (Majide Imi Wakannai).*** "I've no idea what you're saying," or "I simply don't understand."
> ***MM (Maji Mendokusuai).*** Truly irritating.
> ***MM (Maji Mukatsuku).*** "I'm extremely irritated."
> ***MMM (Maji de Mō Muri).*** Totally impossible.

(ERO. Porn.)

Ero is short for *erochikku*, "erotic," and has been a popular word on the Japanese streets since the 1920s.

As a Japanese prefix, it has a similar effect on nouns as the English "porn," "pornographic," "adult," "sex," or "sexy."

Ero adobenchā gēmu. Pornographic adventure game (interactive video game).

Ero anime. Porn anime.

Ero bide. Porn video, porn DVD.

Ero burogu. Sex blog; also commonly shortened into *erogu*.

Erochan (Miss / Young Mr. Erotic). A young, sexy person.

Ero chatto. Sex chat (online), sex chat-room. *Tsūshotto ero*, "two-shot ero," is a one-on-one pornographic chat, usually using a webcam.

Ero daunrōdo. A porn download.

Ero den. Erotic chat-line, phone sex, or an obscene phone-call (which is also called *itaden*).

Ero fantajii. Sexual fantasy.

Ero furasshu gēmu. Porn flash-game.

Ero gazō. Pornographic images.

Erogē. Pornographic computer game.

Erogēmā. Someone who habitually plays pornographic computer games.

Eroguro eiga (erotic grotesque movie). Pornographic splatter movie.

Ero gutsu (erotic goods). XXX merchandise, such as dildos, whips, and so on.

Ero hon. Sex book.

Ero kanchō. Erotic enema.

Ero koi. Sexual love.

Ero keijiban. Erotic bulletin board.

Erokun (young Mr. Erotic). A young sexy guy.

Erokurabu. Sex club.

Ero mikku. A person who uses *mixi,* a major Japanese social networking site, for sexual interaction.
Ero mūbii. Porn movie. Also *ero eizō.*
Ero niku (sex meat). A coarse term for vagina.
Ero omocha. Sex toys.
Eroresu. Erotic wrestling.
Ero rinjērii. Sexy lingerie.
Ero-ri (erotic Lolita). Pedophilia directed at underaged girls.
Ero-rori (ero-Lolita). Young women who dress in provocative baby-doll outfits.
Ero shashin. Pornographic photos.
Ero shitagi. Sexy underwear.

The adjectival form of *ero* is *eroi,* which is also often used in slangy speech to mean "raunchy" or "obscene."

Omae eroi yatsu da zo!
You're so raunchy!
Eroi!
Gross!
Ano hon sugē eroi!
That book's really raunchy!

Another *ero* variation is *erochika,* meaning "sex-freak." The uninitiated bystander might be led to believe that "erotica" is being covertly discussed, but the etymology of this neologism is the phrase *ero ni chikai*—"close to obscenity."

Anna erochika ni sawarasete tamaru ka! Jōdan ja nai!
I'd never let a sex-freak like that touch me! No way!
Anta no otōto 'tte honto no erochika ni natchatta ne!
Your little brother's turned into a total sex-freak!

Erogansu, a fusion of "erotic" and "elegance," is often used for fashion or porn models that are erotic and elegant,

as opposed to erotic and cheap, *erodarashinai* (erotic-sloven-
ly). The *erofueshonaru,* a compound of "erotic" and "professional," is either a pro in the porn business, or someone who
is a pro in bed.

Erokawa, from "erotic," and *kawaii,* "cute," is a girl and
sometimes a boy with an erotic appeal that is not provocative.
They can also be referred to as *erokawa chan,* literally "Miss
Cute Erotic," or *erokawa kun,* "young Mr. Erotic." The acronym
used for erotic-cute women in text messages or in the speech
of young slangsters is *ECO*—short for *erokawa onna.*

In cases where the sex appeal is more scary than appealing, the term *erokowai* (erotic-frightening) is used.

(ESU. S.)

S has had a long and colorful history in Japanese slang. In the
1870s, when the opening of Japan created mass hysteria for
all things Western, the Roman alphabet began to be used as
an exotic code, and there was a particular fascination with the
letter "S," pronounced *esu.* In the early years, S stood for *shan*
or *shen,* both Japanese pronunciations of the German word
schoen, meaning "beautiful." *Kanojo shen,* meaning "She is beautiful," was the rage, and it soon evolved into *Kanojo esu,* "She is
S." In the first two decades of the twentieth century, the next
generation created Anglo-German concoctions like *bakkushen*
(from "back" and *schoen*), originally meaning "nice ass," but
later also "attractive from behind, but what a shock when you
see her from the front." Both these terms were also rendered
as the initials *BS,* pronounced *bii esu.*

In modern times, S has been used in all corners of Japanese
slang:

S for "Escape" (as in *S*-cape)

> **Ano gurūpu kara esu shiyō ze.**
> Let's split from that group.
> **Esu shinai to yabai ze!**
> Let's get the hell outta here!

S for "Smoking"

> **Koko esu eria?**
> Is this a smoking area?
> **Nē! Ima kara esu shinai?**
> You wanna have a smoke now?

S for "Secret"

> **Kono koto esu ni shit'oite yo.**
> Keep that a secret.
> **Kore zettai ni esu dakara ne!**
> This is a total secret, OK!

S for "Sex"

> **Kinō sando esu shita.**
> I had sex three times yesterday.
> **Esu wa dō?**
> How about a little fling?

S for "Sperm"

> **Esu no omorashi.**
> A blob of sperm.
> **'Yada omae! Esu no shimi tsukete! Kondo kara ki o tsukete yo!**
> Hey! You got a cum stain on this! Be more careful next time!

S for "sister," referring among older slang speakers to close friendships among young women that might extend into the realm of lesbianism.

> **Ano ko-tachi itsumo beta beta shite'ru kara, kitto esu yo!**
> Those two girls are always all over each other. They must be "sisters"!
> **Anta-tachi esu ja nai no?**
> You girls are "sisters," right?

In the sex trade and online hookup circles, the letter *S* stands for *skin*, "condom." *Enu-esu* (*NS*) means "no condom." The letters *SF* and *NS* in an online profile indicate that the individual is seeking a "sex friend" for a "no condom" meeting.

S also stands for "sadism." In *esu purei*, "*S* play," customers in sex clubs can humiliate hostesses. Sadists in bondage circles are known as *esu-o*, "*S*-men," and *esu-jo*, "*S*-women."

(ETCHI. H.)

The initial *H*, pronounced *etchi*, is commonly used to judge something or someone as perverse. The *H* stands for the word *hentai* ("abnormal" or "pervert") or *hentaisei* (abnormal sex). "*KYA! Etchi!*" (Oooh, gross!) is a characteristic reaction of horror when one is suddenly confronted with something sexually explicit.

> **Etchi na koto suruna! Omae!**
> Yo! Don't be gross!

To add force to *etchi*, emphatic prefixes like the popular Osaka-dialect *do-* and the prefix *chō-* (super) can be used.

> *Ano kyabasuke do-etchi!*
> That bimbo's a total sleaze!
> *Ano eiga chō-etchi datta yo! Zembu marumie nan da ze!*
> That film was just *so* raunchy! You could see everything!

Etchi suru, "to do *H*," is a very popular term for sexual intercourse, similar to slangy American terms like "getting down and dirty" or "doing the nasty," and *hitori-etchi,* "self-*H*" means "masturbation."

> *Suzuko to etchi shita?*
> Did you lay Suzuko?
> *Etchi shiyō?*
> Shall we get down and dirty?
> *Ken wa kessa kara chatto de hitori-etchi suru?*
> Ken's been jerking off in that chat room since this morning?

Some more variations on *H:*

> *Cha-etchi*, short for *chatto etchi* (chat *H*). An online chat involving masturbation. Also known as *raibuchatt etchi* (live-chat *H*).
> *Denwa etchi* (phone *H*). Telephone sex.
> *Etchi bideo.* Porn movies (video or DVD). Also *etchibide* for short.
> *Etchi dibidi.* Porn DVD.
> *Etchi shiin.* Sex scene.
> *Etchi shōsetsu.* Pornographic novel.
> *Etchi tomodachi* (*H* friend), usually shortened to *etchitomo,* means "sex friend" or "fuck buddy." It is also often used in its anglicized versions *Etchi furendo,* and the shorter *etchifure.*
> *Etchi shame.* Short for *etchi shashin mēru* (*H*-picture e-mail). X-rated pictures and snapshots (usually of oneself) sent as e-mail attachments or by cell phone.

Mēru-etchi (mail *H*). Masturbatory e-mail exchange or text messaging.

Sukaipu etchi. (Skype *H*). Using Skype for X-rated interaction.

Tsūshotto etchi (two-shot *H*). Cam-to-cam cybersex.

(FERA. Fellatio.)

Japanese words for fellatio fit into two groups: foreign imports favored by the modern crowd, and domestic words favored by the maturer, or at least more traditional, slang users.

Of the two groups, the foreign words (all of them now American or American-inspired) are gaining ground as, to Japanese ears, they have the triple advantage of being naughty, exotic, and ultrafashionable.

If you look up "fellatio" in an up-to-date Japanese dictionary, *ferachio*, the Japanese transliteration of "fellatio," might come first. Then comes the obsolete and therefore inoffensive Japanese term *kyūkei*, which is made up of the characters for "suck" and "stem," followed by a punctilious explanation like *Danseiki ni taisuru seppun*, "kissing of the male sexual organ." In Japan today, the most widely understood word for fellatio is *fera*, a Japanese contraction of the English word. Often you will hear it in the form of *ofera*, the honorific o- added as a linguistic shock-absorber.

> **Kono bā de hosutesu no fera no sābisu ari ka yo?**
> Do the girls at this bar offer fellatio service?
> **Watashi ofera daisuki!**
> I love sucking dick!

Today *fera* appears in many combinations:

Bakyūmufera (vacuum fellatio). Fellatio with much suction.
Ferari (Ferrari). A pun on the car model.
Ferasābisu (fellatio service). Offered in sex clubs.
Ferasha (fellatio pic). Short for *fera shashin*, "fellatio photograph."
Ferashame (fellatio picture e-mail). An e-mail attachment of a photograph portraying fellatio.
Gomufera (rubber fellatio). Fellatio with a condom.
Osōjifera (cleaning fellatio). The penis is licked after the man has ejaculated.
Niodachifera (daunting-pose fellatio). Fellatio with the man standing with legs akimbo.
Nuttorifera (soggy fellatio). Fellatio with much spittle.

A popular word for fellatio in some sex clubs is *kyandē*, inspired by the English word "candy."

Suzuko no kyandē wa saikō!
Suzuko's blow jobs are the best!
Sakku nashi kyandē wa gomen yo!
No condom—no blow job!

Many of Japan's sex clubs have developed extraordinary fellatio techniques that appear on their "menus" under exotic American names. *Kokku-sakkingu*, "cock sucking"; *kokku-sakkingu purē*, "cock-sucking play"; or *kokku-sakkingu gēmu*, "cock-sucking game," for instance, imply a fellatio technique often performed with the hostess' mouth full of liquor. Other American-inspired expressions for fellatio like *ōraru sekkusu*, "oral sex," or *furūto*, "flute," are gaining popularity on the sex-club scene. *Nama* (raw) is the term for condomless service, while hostesses who use condoms on their customers have developed titillating techniques that come under the heading of *ofera kabuse*, "fellatio with cover."

(GENNAMA. Money.)

When cash or money is discussed in everyday Japanese life, basic words like *okane,* "money"; *genkin,* "ready money"; or *kyasshu,* "cash," are used. On the streets, however, Yakuza jargon and slang favored by underworld cliques offer a colorful assortment of idioms inaccessible to the foreigner and even to the average Japanese.

Today the word *gennama* lies on the borderline of respectability, although until after World War II, only the street crowd would have known or used it. Etymologically, it comes from *gen* (money), and *nama* (raw or fresh). It originated as an *ingo* (secret Yakuza slang) word during the Meiji period (1868–1912) and led an underground existence until it entered popular usage through the cops-and-robbers films of the 1950s and 60s.

> *Gennama ima motte koi!*
> Hand over the cash now!

Many of the other words for money in use today on the streets and in the underworld originated in the Meiji period or the Taisho period (1912–26). Words like *ura,* "back"; *tsura,* "face"; *higo,* "protection"; *riki,* "convenience"; and *watari,* "handing over," have remained street lingo used exclusively by thieves and pickpockets.

> *Ore no ura dakara!*
> That's my dough!
> *Tsura motte'ru?*
> Got any moola?
> *Omae no higo iranē zo!*
> I don't need your fuckin' cash!
> *Sono riki ore ni watasanē to, buchikorosu zo!*
> If you don't hand over the *dinero*, I'll beat the shit outta you!
> *Shimpai suru na! Watari o tsukete kite yaru kara!*
> Don't worry! I'm gonna get the bread together!

Another word popular on the streets is the mysterious *ru*, as in:

> *Ru motte'ru?*
> You got the cash?
> *Ru chōdai!*
> Gimme the money!

Few users of this short, elusive word know its interesting background. The word that inspired *ru* was *nagare*, meaning "flowing stream" or "current" (the idea being that cash can flow like water). The ideogram for *nagare* has more than one pronounciation; *nagare* is the *kun yomi*, or native Japanese reading, while the *on yomi*, or Chinese reading, gives us the obscure *ru*, a perfect candidate for a discreet code.

The exotic-sounding term *tsūpin* belongs to the same family of underground slang. It originated as a fusion of *tsūka*, "currency," and *pin*, "money."

> *Omae no tsūpin nante iranē!*
> I don't need your loot!
> *Tsūpin yokose yo! Soshitara ii butsu yaru ze!*
> You give us cash, we give you good stuff!
> *Ken ni tsūpin o yattara, sayōnara datta wa yo.*
> After I gave him my dough, Ken walked out on me.

Counterfeit money is known as *nisegane,* "fake money," or *nisesatsu,* "fake bill."

> ***Ano baka yarō! Yaku to hikikae ni nisegane***
> ***tsukamaseyagatte!***
> This fuckin' asshole gave us fake cash for the dope!
> ***Shimpai suruna yo! Kono nisesatsu tsukaeru ze!***
> Don't worry! We can use the fake bills!

Bundles of fake notes (usually the top bill is real and the rest is plain paper) are known on the streets as *anko,* "bean jam," from the Japanese bean-jam buns that look like plain buns but have bean jam hidden inside.

> ***Kore anko ja nai ka! Baka ni suru no mo ii kagen ni shiro!***
> Man! This is paper! Don't fuckin' fuck with me!
> ***Hayaku koko zurakorō ze! Aitsu-ra ga anko ni ki ga tsu-***
> ***ku mae ni na!***
> Let's get the fuck outta here before they catch on it's fake!

(GŌKAN. Rape.)

Gōkan is one of the few formal but direct words that can be used in standard speech when referring to rape. Still, many people believe that it is too strong to be tactfully usable. *Gōkan suru* means "to rape someone," while *gōkan sareru* means "to get raped."

> ***Kanojo wa kako ni gōkan sureta, nigai keiken o motte'ru.***
> She was raped, and has never really got over it.
> ***Kanojo wa gōkan sarete irai seishin ijo ni ochiitte'ru.***
> Since she was raped, she's been having problems.

Other formal words for rape, less used in conversation than *gōkan,* are *kanin,* its verb form *kanin suru,* and *tegome,* which is written either with the characters "hand" and "plunge," or "hand" and "cage." *Tegome* is parallel to the English term "violation," and also usually implies robbery. Nowadays, however, the English-derived *rēpu* is the term most frequently used in conversation.

> **Senshū kono kinjo de futari mo onna ga rēpu sareta yo.**
> Last week two women got raped in this neighborhood.
> **Nani? Aitsu honto ni rēpu shita'tte? Omae honki de itten no?**
> What? He actually raped her? Are you serious?

In order to avoid a direct reference to rape, *osowareru*, "to get attacked" can be used. It is the most commonly used euphemism.

> **Uchi no imōto ichinen mae osowareta.**
> My sister got raped last year.
> **Kare wa Suzuko o osotta.**
> He raped Suzuko.

A term that needs to be used more carefully is the trenchant *okasu*, "to violate."

> **Aitsu wa onna okashite, satsu ni tsukamatta.**
> The police nabbed him, 'cause he raped this woman.

A graphic word used either for rape, or rough sex, is *hegasu*, "to rip someone's clothes off."

> **Kinō uchi no yatsu o mechakucha hegashite, tanoshinjatta yo!**
> I really fucked my old woman's brains out yesterday! Man, it was great!

Another violent term for rape is *kojiakeru*, meaning "to wrench open." It is also one of the more savage words in Japanese for sexual intercourse.

> **Kanojo no mono o kojiakete yatta!**
> I screwed the shit outta her!

A rapist is officially called a *gōkanhan*, "rape perpetrator." The English-derived *rēpisuto*, "rapist," is also used. In criminal cliques, however, the rapist is called *mamedorobo*, "bean robber," and *mamedori*, "bean snatcher"—*mame* (bean) being a street word for clitoris, but also vagina.

A traditional Yakuza word for rapist is *suzume*, "sparrow."

(GŌTŌ. Robber, burglary.)

A vague but forceful word that the average Japanese and the media use to refer to either violent situations such as holdups, burglary, and housebreaking, or the actual gunman, burglar, or housebreaker.

> **Gōtō ga haitte, heya o mechakucha ni shita!**
> A robber broke in, and turned the whole apartment upside down!
> **Gōtō ga atashi-tachi no mono zembu totte itchatta no yo! Ze-embu yo!**
> This thief took everything we had! Ee-verything!

Ginkō gōtō ("bank robber" or "bank robbery"); *kenjū gōtō* (a "gunman" or a "holdup"); or *hōseki gōtō* (jewel thief) are some of the possible combinations you can come across.

When criminals get together to talk shop, ordinary words like "thief" or "robber" prove too colorless and broad. "What do you mean by 'thief'?" the confused specialist will ask. "Do you mean a push-up ghee, a lush roller, a second-story man, a spider, a chainman, or are we discussing a worm-walker?"

The Japanese criminal world is just as elaborate as its American counterpart when it comes to criminal job descriptions. Some of the types of thieves and the cognomens that *ingo* (criminal language) initiates use in chatting about each other are:

Agari, the "ascender," the individual who specializes in cat burglary.

Aki, "vacant," the thief who will target a home only if its inhabitants are out.

Akinaishi, "trade expert," the master thief who has developed his art to a finely tuned perfection.

Akisu, "snooper," the stealthy, superdiscreet purloiner.

Anatsutai, "hole-enterer," refers to thieves generally, or more specifically to one who specializes in breaking and entering by making a hole in the outside wall.

Asarifumi, "hunt step," the individual who specializes in stealing from unattended store counters.

Garasuhazushi, the "glass remover," specializes in the removal of glass in windows or doors as a mode of breaking and entering.

Genkanarashi, the "front-door smasher," less subtle than the "glass remover."

Gui, a criminal argot word for accomplice, inspired by the term *tagui*, "of the same kind."

Ichimaimono, "one person," the type of criminal who works alone, with no accomplices or gang affiliations.

Inaori, the "threatener," usually used for a mugger.

Iri, "entering," is another *ingo* (hidden language) synonym for thief.

Itafumi, "floor step," the thief who specializes in public-bath and sauna locker-rooms. The root of this word, *ita*, "floor" or "floorboard," is used with various suffixes to create synonyms for locker-room thieves such as *itabashiri*, the "floor runner," or *itanomikasegi*, "floorboard labor" (in Osakan dialect, *itabakasegi*).

Kaikuri, a train thief whose method is to exchange bags that look alike.

Kajidoro, "fire thief," can be either an individual who sets fire to the place he intends to rob in order to take advantage of the commotion, or a thief who is quick to act during natural disasters.

Kanebako, "money box," a thief who works on trains. (*Bako*, "box," is criminal argot for train.)

Kanekuchi, "money mouth," refers to the coin receptacle of a public telephone, and by extension to a small-time thief whose forte is ripping off phone booths.

Kanetataki, "money beater," a mugger. This type of criminal will approach his victim in the street and threaten to "beat the money" out of him unless he hands it over. The shortened version, *tataki*, is also commonly used.

Kerikomi, the "kick enterer," a synonym for burglar. If in English a burglar "breaks and enters," the *kerikomi* "kicks and enters."

Kumo, "spider," a cat burglar, or in American criminal slang, a "spider."

Kyakushitsunerai, "guest-room aimer," a thief who targets hotels, specializing in removing valuables from the rooms.

Nobi is another synonym for cat burglar, inspired by the verb *nobiru*, "to climb in."

Obu, "hot bath," a public-bath or locker-room thief.

Ohiki is the accomplice of a shoplifter who creates a diversion so his partner will be free to work.

Okkake is a word for mugger that came originally from the Tochigi dialect. It was inspired by the verb *oikakeru*, "to follow."

Osae, the "restrainer," the aggressive burglar who will stop at nothing to get at the goods.

Oshiiri, "pushing and entering," is another variation on the individual who breaks and enters.

> **Oshikomi**, "pushing with force," is a synonym for the rob-
> ber who pushes his or her way forcefully into a residence.
> **Otenkinagashi**, the "weather criminal," the person who
> stands watch outside while his friends are inside looting.
> **Sewanuki** is a word used for the robber who stalks night-
> time streets and bars looking for inebriated individuals.
> This expression is made up of *sewa*, "to help," and *nuku*, "to
> pull out," since this thief holds out a "helping hand."
> **Shiro usagi**, the "white rabbit," or just plain *usagi*, "rabbit,"
> is an appellation reserved for the petty criminal. In olden
> days, the "rabbit" thief would limit himself to stealing
> vegetables from the fields; today the expression has broad-
> ened to include all criminals who aim for minor targets.
> **Zumburi**, "from top to bottom," the locker-room thief who
> methodically cleans out locker rooms.

(GUDŌ. Tools of the trade.)

Depending on the job, there is an array of specialized tools a
criminal might take along—tools ranging from coils, widgets,
and jiggers, to guns, metal bats, and flamethrowers. *Gudō* is the
standard *ingo* (criminal slang) word for the tools of the trade.
Gudō has the typical *ingo* characteristic of being an inverted
word, in this case of the standard word *dogū*, "tool."

Some of the typical *gudō* on the backstreets of Japan are:

> **Ara**, "knife," originated in the adjective *araarashii*, "rough"
> or "violent." Its American equivalents are "blade"
> and "chopper."
> **Ate**, "objective," is the wrench or blade used for breaking in.
> **Bāru**, "crowbar." Also *kanabō*, "iron rod," and *kanateko*,
> "iron lever."
> **Chōshinki**, "stethoscope," for cracking safes.
> **Dosu** is a dagger used by the Yakuza.

Emma is a word for the pincers used for picking locks, or for other operations requiring delicacy.

Gasujū, "gas gun," is tear gas or another noxious-gas shooter.

Hajiki, from the verb *hajiku*, "to flick" or "to flip," is the favorite street word for gun. Other popular words for gun in crime jargon are *chakka, kenji, tandzutsu,* and *teikurō.* The official terms are *shōkaki,* "small firearm"; *teppo,* "gun"; and *kenjō,* literally "fist pistol." *Gan,* the English word "gun," and *pisutoru,* "pistol," are also often used.

Kaebin, "flame pot," is a Molotov cocktail.

Kaenhōshaki, "flamethrower."

Kanejū is the special fine wire used for prying locks open. The word evolved from the character for *hari,* "needle," which is made up of two components. If you break the character apart, the left component is *kane* (metal) and the right component is *jū* (ten).

Kani, "crab," is the word for a small pair of scissors useful for snipping through bag straps or cutting into outside pockets to reach concealed valuables.

Kattanaifu, "cutter knife," is a box cutter used as a weapon or cutting tool.

Kinzokubatto, "metal bat," used as a tool for smashing and entering, or as a defense weapon.

Mame, "beans," means "bullets."

Merikensakku, "knuckle busters," are brass knuckles.

Oisore, "at a moment's notice," is a sharp little knife that can be used for all types of thieving, not to mention being handy as a weapon of defense.

Ōto or **ōtomachikku**, "automatic," is the firearm that some criminals carry just in case. Its ungainly official name is *jidōshikikenju.*

Pachinko is an older gangster word for gun. It was inspired by *pachinko,* the Japanese pinball game, the loud banging sound of the machines suggesting gunfire. In criminal circles, a shoot-out is called *donpachi.*

Renkon, "lotus root," is a revolver, and a *karashi renkon*, "mustard lotus-root," or *karashi* for short, is a Kalashnikov. *Karashi* (mustard) is a pun on the Japanese pronunciation of "Kalashnikov," *karashinikobu*.

Saka is a knife of any shape or size that might be found in a Japanese thief's black box, used for anything from cutting and prying things open to self-defense. The word *saka* was inspired by Osaka, a city renowned for the quality of its knives.

Shippiki is a sharp precision tool convenient for picking locks.

Shūryūdan and **teryūdan**, both literally meaning "hand-pomegranate bullet," are hand grenades, as are *tenage-dama*, "hand-thrown bullets"; *senkōdama*, "flash bullets"; and *sutanguranēdo*, "stun grenades."

Unagi, "eel," is a thin rope useful in a variety of breaking-and-entering situations.

(HAKO. Vagina.)

Many words for vagina in the darker alleys of the Japanese street scene depict it as a receptacle. *Hako*, "box," is an example of just one of the taboo terms that were created after dark when the boys got together for drinks and a bit of conversation.

> ***Ato, hako yari ni ikō ka?***
> You wanna get us some pussy after this?
> ***Atarashii sutorippā no hako mita? Sugē!***
> Did you see the new stripper's box? Hot!

After a hard day at work, it is customary for male workers in Japan to hit the scene, while wives and girlfriends stay at home. The relaxed and predominantly masculine tone of such "boys on the town" outings often inspires intimate discussions that become franker as the men become more sloshed. When these conversations call for either a precise differentiation among vaginas or an accurate description of a particular vagina, the dishes on the table, the bowls of food, the sake cups, and the other restaurant utensils have all proved excellent analogies for organs of every shape, size, and color.

The *sara* or *ōzara* are large, shallow dishes that can be used to refer to vaginas that are wide but not deep.

> *Ore don don tsukimakutte, kanojo no sara no kabe made itchimatta.*
> I pushed my way in deeper and deeper until I hit her sugar-walls.
> *Suzuko no ōzara wa Roppongi ja saikō da ze!*
> Suzuko has the best twat in Roppongi!

The vagina of a young girl or virgin can be referred to as *atarabachi*, "new pot," or *ochoko*, "small sake cup."

> *Kanojo no atarabachi shimatte'ru!*
> Her little snatch is real tight!
> *Omae no ochoko de yarashite kure yo na!*
> Come let me play with your little pussy!

A vagina that is deep and easily penetrable by a penis can be called *ohachi*, "deep bowl," or *suribachi*, an earthenware mortar.

> *Ore kanojo no ohachi ni muriyari irekondara, mō tengoku datta ze!*
> When I plunged deep into her crack, it was heaven!
> *Washi no onna wa suribachi no tsukaikata o yoku shitte oru!*
> My woman really knows how to work that love-muscle!

Other receptacles popular as bawdy synonyms for vagina are *utsuwa*, "container," and *meiki*, "vase." *Meiki* is used to specify a top-quality vagina, and has become so popular as a sexual slang word that its original meaning of "vase" has been all but forgotten.

> *Ore no mono o iretara, kanojo no utsuwa piku piku furuwasete'ta!*
> When I put it in, her cunt started quivering!
> *Omae kanojo no meiki ni yubi o tsukkonda'tte? Temē na!*
> You put your finger up her snatch! You dog!

(HAMERU. To put in.)

Hameru belongs to a group of words that should be used with caution as they have strong sexual undertones. *Botan o hamenasai!* "Do your buttons up!" or *Tebukuro o hamenasai!* "Wear your gloves!" are everyday idiomatic expressions. The danger lies in that *Hamenasai!* can just as well be interpreted to mean "Stick it in me!" or "Give it to me!"

> *Hamete chōdai!*
> Fuck me!
> *Hajimete dendokokeshi o hamete mitara, sugokatta!*
> When I stuck a vibrator in for the first time, it was great.

To create a slightly stronger synonym, *komu,* which suggests entering with force, can be added to *hameru,* creating *hamekomu.*

> *Fukaku hamekonde chōdai!*
> Ram it in deep!
> *Nē! Anta hamekomu toki, mō chotto yasashīku shite kuretara ii no ni!*
> I wish you'd be a bit gentler when you stick it in!

Another risque word is *sōnyū,* literally "insertion." Handle with care, for despite its being a formal dictionary word, it can be used in a slangy context with more impact than *hameru* or *hamekomu.* Its two characters are *sō,* meaning "put in," and *nyū,* meaning "enter."

> *Tampon o sōnyū suru.*
> To insert a tampon.
> *Kare ga gin no sōnyū shite kita!*
> He inserted his pulsating meat!

The next rung down on the ladder of roughness brings us to *tsukkomu,* which literally means "to thrust into" or "to plunge into" (the character *tsuku* means "to stab," and *komu* means "into").

Tsukkomu can be used in everyday speech in combinations like *Poketto ni te o tsukkonda,* "He thrust his hands into his pockets"—but be advised that the average Japanese will make an immediate association with sexual thrusting.

> ***Chimpo o tsukkonda.***
> He thrust his dick in.
> ***Kanojo no kuchi ni tsukkonjatta!***
> He thrust it into her mouth!

To add even more force to *tsuku,* the suffix *-makuru* (over and over), which originated in the dialects of the Kansai region but is now popular all over Japan, is often added, creating *tsukimakuru,* "to stab again and again."

> ***Anta! Itsumade mo tsukimakutte!***
> Baby! Keep shoving it in forever!
> ***Doa ga aita toki, ore kanojo no ana ni tsukimakutte'ta!***
> I was hammering away at her when the door opened!

The harshest of these six technical terms is *bukkomu.* The character for this word is *butsu,* meaning to "hit," and *komu,* meaning "into."

> ***Fukaku oku made bukkonde!***
> Ram it in all the way!
> ***Atashi kare ga ikisō ni naru no wakaru'n da yo nē! Sugē ikioi de bukkomu kara sā!***
> I can always tell when he's about to come 'cause he starts humping away like crazy!

(HE. Breaking wind.)

This is a straightforward, down-to-earth term, like the English word "fart." Unlike its English equivalent, however, *he* has a reputable literary background. It is related to the formal word *hōhi*, the expression favored by Japanese authors throughout the ages when they felt the need to mention farts in respectable literary works.

The character *hō* stands for "sending out" (as in *hōsō*, "to broadcast"), and *hi* signifies "air" or "wind." The indigenous reading of the character *hi* is *he*, which has become one of the most popular terms for fart.* In everyday usage, *hiru*, "to flutter," and *suru*, "to do," are added to make *he* into a verb:

> ***Dare ga he o hitta?***
> Who farted?
> ***Ima he shita'n deshō? Aa! Mō! Kusai jan!***
> You just farted, right? Oh, no! What a stink!

The ever-popular Osaka dialect has donated its own bawdy variations to mainstream Japanese with the verbs *koku*, "to do"; *tareru*, "to drop"; and *kamasu*, "to stink up."

> ***He o koita.***
> He let one rip.
> ***He o tareta.***
> He let one go.
> ***He o kamushita.***
> He cracked a fart.

---

*A scandalous haiku by the medieval master poet Sōkan (ca. 1464–ca. 1552) goes:

Waga oya no	Even as my father
Shinuru toki ni mo	Lay dying
He o kokite	I farted

The Osaka dialect, cherished in Japan for its liveliness, has further contributed fart-related words like *hetare* and *hekoki*, both literally meaning "farter," but generally used to accuse someone of idiocy.

> **Ano hetare ore no kane nusunda!**
> That idiot stole my money!
> **Nanka monku aru no ka? Hekoki!**
> So what's your problem, idiot?

Related to *he* is the comical word *sukashippe*, which refers to a silent fart. It was created from *sukashi*, "transparent," with *pe* used in place of *he* to facilitate pronunciation.

> **Sukashippe o suru tsumori datta ga, oto dashichatta.**
> I was gonna fart discreetly, but I really let one rip.
> **Dōshite mo gaman ga dekinakunatchatte, sukashippe o shichatta!**
> I just couldn't hold back, so I let one fly!

A type of fart especially popular among small Japanese schoolboys is the *nigirippe*. *Nigiru* means "to clasp" or "to hold tight," and *pe* (from *he*) is "fart." The technique involves farting into one's clenched fist and then quickly holding one's hand up to one's friend's nose.

> **Mattaku ano chibigaki! Ichinichijū nigirippe shite! Komatta!**
> That nasty little brat! He's been passing farts around all day!
> **Mata nigirippe shitara, anta no shiri tataku yo!**
> If I ever see you pull that little fart trick again, I'll spank your bottom!

A synonym for *nigirippe* is *tsukambe*, literally "catching the fart," an expression originating in the Tohoku dialects.

> **Uchi no otō-san tondemonai yo! Mata tsukambe shite sā!**
> My dad's so gross! He's constantly passing around farts!
> **Mō sono toshi ni natte, tsukambe nanka shinaide yo! Ojii-chan!**
> C'mon, grandpa! Still doing that fart-in-hand trick at your age?

Quite a few proverbs use farts as their subject matter. These proverbs are always fun, although one must be careful as to when and where they are used.

> **He o koite, shiri o subomu.**
> Having farted, he closed his ass.

This refers to the wrongdoer who, after an indiscretion, assumes a nonchalant air.

> **Itachi no saigobe.**
> A weasel's final fart.

This refers to a last desperate action, the belief being that a hunted weasel at the end of its tether will fart into its pursuer's face, hoping that the shock will enable it to escape. It also refers to a person who upon being fired—having nothing more to lose—speaks his or her mind.

> **He hitotsu wa kusuri sempuku ni mukau.**
> One fart is worth a thousand pills.

This is the motto of a Japanese granny. A loose translation would be, "A fart a day keeps the doctor away."

The other word ranking with *he* in popularity is *onara*. *O-* is a softening, honorific prefix, and *nara* means "sound," as in *narasu*, "to ring, sound, or blow."

> **Ōkii na onara o shite shimatta!**
> He really let one rip!
> **Daiji na kaigichū ni onara shichatta!**
> He farted right in the middle of an important conference!

Another popular word for fart is *būbū*. It conveys rumbling gastric sounds—the onomatopoeic expression *būbū iu* means "to complain." The equally onomatopoeic *būbū suru,* however, means "to fart," so be careful in choosing the right verb.

> **Onara būbū suru.**
> To fart sonorously.
> **Onara būbū suruna yo! Kusē darō!**
> Man! Don't fart, it stinks!

Another crass but cheerful word for farting is *būsuka*.

> **Omae beddo no naka de busuka suruna yo! Kusakute tamannē yo!**
> Don't fart in the bed! God, it stinks!
> **Ojii-chan'ttara! Onegai dakara! Okyaku-san no iru toki busuka shinaide chōdai!**
> Grandpa! Please! I wish you wouldn't fart when we have guests!

You can repeat *būsuka* twice in order to give a break-wind description the extra edge.

> **Onara o būsuka būsuka shita.**
> He let one rip.

(HERO. Heroin.)

Over the years, Japanese heroin-smugglers, dealers, users, and the cliques they associate with have created an exclusive vocabulary rich in synonyms. Special words were created to define the drug's quality and potency, to characterize the different people that come in contact with it, and to name the paraphernalia needed to consume it.

Hero, a contraction of "heroin," is a popular slang word that everyone understands.

> **Hero o utsu.**
> To shoot up heroin.
> **Hero o kagu.**
> To snort heroin.
> **Hero yatta koto aru?**
> Ever done any heroin?

Drug cliques more than any other group on the edges of society need a private jargon to confuse eavesdropping outsiders. A common trick in Japanese slang is the inversion of words in order to make them incomprehensible. As *hero* was never much of a secret, *rohe* often took its place.

> **Kon'ya rohe o shiireyō ze!**
> Let's go shopping for some dope tonight!
> **Hayaku rohe o shiirete konakya!**
> I need to get my hands on some dope quickly!

Following international trends in drug lingo, the next logical degree of contraction after *hero* would be *H* (pronounced *eichi*) or *he*. This proved difficult in Japan, as *H* (pronounced *etchi*) is a popular slang term for sex or pervert. As *he* is equally inappropriate—it means "fart"—the consensus settled on *pe* as the preferred clandestine form.

> **Sukoshi pe o yarō ze!**
> C'mon, let's do some *H*!
> **Ken mata pe sū?**
> Ken's smoking *H* again?

Two synonyms for heroin that are also frequently inverted are *kona*, "flour," which can become *nako*, and *tane*, "seed," which can become *neta*.

> *Ano kona doko de te ni ireta no?*
> Where did you get hold of that snow?
> *Nako ichikiro mitsuyu shita.*
> I smuggled in a kilo of stuff.
> *Sono neta to hoka no mon' mikkusu shinē hō ga mi no tame da ze! Oboeteru darō, Ken no koto?*
> Don't mix this *H* with other stuff! Remember what happened to Ken?
> *Omē tane sutte'ru no ka yo?? Utta hō ga yoppodo kiku'n da ze!*
> You smoke this stuff?? You get more outta shooting it up!

High quality *neta* can be referred to as *mabuneta*, "pretty seed," or in specific reference to heroin, *nambā yon*, "number four."

> *Oi! Kore sugē mabuneta ja nē ka! Ore . . . mō . . . mero mero!*
> Man! This stuff's awesome! Wow! I'm really fucked-up!
> *Ore ga sabaite'ru no wa nambā yon dake da ze!*
> I only sell number-four stuff!

Dealers are called *motojime*, "promoters"; *oroshimoto*, "wholesale source"; and *netamoto*, "drug source." On the street, heroin is measured by grams—the usual one-gram quantity as *G*, pronounced *jii*; anything beyond that is counted in the usual form: *ni guramu*, "two grams"; *san guramu*, "three grams"; and so on.

> *Hero jii katta yo.*
> I bought a gram of *H*.
> *Ima pe ni guramu ikura?*
> How much is two grams of *H* now?

The favorite indirect reference to heroin is *butsu*, "thing"; other fashionable euphemisms are *shiro*, "white"; *matsu* and *funmatsu,* "powder"; and *yuki,* "snow," all of which can also be used to refer to cocaine or other white, powdery drugs. *Shirochan,* "Little Miss White," is also used.

> **Kono butsu hitofukuro sabakitai.**
> I wanna sell this bag of stuff.
> **Dare ka shiro utte'ru?**
> Anyone selling *H*?
> **Ki o tsukero! Ano matsu dame da!**
> Be careful, man! This sugar's bogus!
> **Ano fummatsu ima yaru?**
> You gonna do this powder now?
> **Kinō no yuki warukatta! Honto ni byōki ni natchatta!**
> That snow yesterday was bad! I really got sick!

Along with other hard drugs, heroin is often referred to as *kusuri,* "medicine," or in its inverted form, *sukuri.*

> **Omē ki o tsuketa hō ga ii ze! Kono kusurui saiaku da!**
> You'd better be careful! This stuff's bogus!
> **Kono sukuri sugē usumete atte! Zenzen kikanē jan!**
> This stuff's too diluted! I don't feel shit!

Other inversions of *kusuri,* popular because they are also puns, are *risuki,* "risk"; *kurisu,* "Chris"; and *suriku,* "slick."

> **Sono supūn yokose yo! Risuku no jikan da!**
> Hand me the spoon! It's time to fix the stuff!
> **Ano kurisu ippatsu de buttonda ze! Ore nanka hikari ni tsutsumarete shimatta ze!**
> One shot of this and I was flying! I was really tripping!*
> **Omae sonna boroi chūshaki de suriku utsu ki ka yo!**
> You're not gonna shoot up with that fucked-up needle, are you?

---

*Literally, "I was covered with lights."

Syringes are generally called *orenjibōshi*, "orange hat," and *orepen*, short for "orange pen"—as many of Japan's Terumo Corporation's syringes have orange pumps.

(HEROCHŪ. Heroin addict.)

The correct term for heroin addict is *heroin chūdokusha*, which is avoided on the streets in favor of shorter, slangier expressions.

In the twenties, the word *aruchū*, for alcoholic, appeared on the Japanese scene (from *arukōru chūdoku*, "alcohol addiction"). When heroin usage increased, this term inspired the word *herochū*, a contraction of *heroin chūdoku*, "addicted to heroin," which has remained one of the most popular slang terms for the heroin addict.

> *Ano herochū no ude wa akai hanten darake.*
> That smack-slammer's arm is full of red marks.
> *Ken wa herochū? Shiranakatta!*
> Ken's a dopehead? I didn't know that!

Two other words for heroin junkie are *herokan* (from *heroin kanja*, "heroin patient") and *pekan* (*pe* is short for "heroin").

> *Ore no dachi wa minna herokan dakara.*
> My friends are all a bunch of junkies.
> *Kono manshon wa pekan-tachi darake!*
> This building is full of heroin addicts!

Other favorites for heroin junkie are *pechū*, from *heroin chūdoku* (addicted to heroin), and *peboke*, from *pe* (heroin) and *boke* (muddled).

> *Kono butsu o pechū no dachi kara te ni ireta.*
> I got this stuff from a junkie friend of mine.

Japanese antidrug laws are very harsh. Heroin addicts are much more careful than their American peers about where they buy the drug and where they consume it. Special apartments or "pads" where heroin can be bought and used in a safe environment are known as *hero kutsu* or *pe kutsu*, with *kutsu* being short for *dōkutsu*, "cavern."

> ***Ore sugē ii herokutsu shitte'ru kara, itte yarō ze!***
> I know a good pad where we can go and shoot up!
> ***Na! Ima sugu yo! Pe kutsu ikō ze! Ore, yo! Ima, yo!***
> ***Hitouchi hitsuyō nan da yo!***
> Man, hurry up! Quick, come on, let's hit the den! Man, I need a fix!

(HIMO. Pimp.)

A procurer is formally known in Japanese as a *haishun assen gyōsha* (literally, "prostitute-mediator-tradesman"). Not an easy word to get one's tongue around, which is why on the streets and in everyday speech the preferred expression is *himo*. *Himo* literally means "string" or "rope," the idea being that pimps "rope" the girls in and "tie" them to their work.

This term dates back to the days of the *aosen*, "blue-line," and *akasen*, "red-line," districts, before prostitution was made illegal in 1958. The blue-line district was the officially designated area of town where licensed prostitutes and their pimps could legally work, while the red-line district housed the unlicensed women.

> ***Tokyo de himo no seikatsu o shite'ru.***
> He's working as a pimp in Tokyo.
> ***Ore Ken ga himo da nante, shiranakatta ze! Yaru jan!***
> I didn't know Ken was a pimp! Wild!

A prostitute who works for a pimp is known on the streets as *himotsuki,* "pimp-attached."

> **Kono bā no onna wa minna himotsuki.**
> All the girls in this bar work with pimps.

Some Tokyo women, who support their poorer, unproductive boyfriends, refer to them playfully as *himo.*

> **Atashi no himo ga ne! Motto kane kure'tte iu no yo ne!**
> You know that guy of mine! He wants more money again!
> **Atashi no ima made no himo'tte, ii kao wa shite'n da yo nē, minna!**
> All my boyfriends have always been pretty but poor!

In the sex trade, pimps prefer to be called *manējā,* "manager," or *pōtā,* "porter," but do not take kindly to being called *himo,* which is as uncomplimentary as the English "pimp."

> **Anta no manējā dare?**
> Who's your dude?
> **Aitsu Ōsaka de pōtā yatte, hitomōke shita ze!**
> He made a bundle working as a pimp in Osaka!

Another popular word for pimp is *pombiki.* Since pimping in the traditional sense is illegal in Japan today, the modern *pombiki* stands outside different red-light establishments trying to boost his income by luring in as many customers as possible. (He gets paid per capita.)

> **Pombiki de ikura ni naru ka na?**
> I wonder how much a pimp makes here?
> **Kono hen no pombiki'tte honto ni shitsukoi ze!**
> **Hipparikomō to suru mon na!**
> The macks around here are so pushy! They like to pull you off the street!

The English-inspired equivalent to *pombiki* is *kachi* (catch).

> **Atarashii kyatchiman dō ka ne? Tsukaeru ka ne?**
> How's the new dude we hired? Any use?
> **Shitsukoi kyatchiman ni wa ki o tsukero yo.**
> Be careful of the pushy pimps.

A comical word for pimp was inspired by Shakespeare's *The Merchant of Venice*. *Benisu*, "Venice," was slightly altered to create *penisu*, "penis," resulting in *penisu no shōnin*, "the merchant of penis," that is, the pimp.

> **Kono hen penisu no shōnin ga kane o kassegimakutte'ru!**
> Man! The pimps in this area must really be raking in the money!
> **Omē koko de nani yatte'n da yo? Penisu no shōnin ka?**
> What are you doing around here? You selling women or something?

(HIROPON. Methamphetamine.)

In Japanese, amphetamines, methamphetamines, and every kind of speed are generally called *kakuseizai*, "awakening medicine." The most popular, methamphetamines, are also known by their original Japanese brand-name *hiropon*, from the Greek *philoponia*, "industriousness" or "eagerness to work." In drug circles, *hiropon* is shortened to *pon*, and also appears as the upbeat *ponzu*, "pickled pon."

> **Aitsu-ra kakuseizai mitsuyu de taiho sareta.**
> They got arrested for smuggling in speed.
> **Pon ippon utsu no ikura?**
> How much is a shot of speed?

While Western amphetaminists tend to "pop" the drug in pill form, in Japan it is often injected—a process called *tsuki,* "moon." Syringes in meth circles are known as *P* for *pompu,* "pump"; *SP* for *supiido pompu,* "speed pump"; and *terumo,* from the Terumo Corporation, Japan's largest manufacturer of medical supplies.

> **Hiropon o utsu.**
> To shoot up amphetamines.
> **Kare no ude wa hiropon de fukureagatte'ru.**
> His arm's really fucked-up from all those speed injections.

Other popular words for various types of speed and amphetamine are:

> **Aisu,** "ice," for crystal meth, which is also called *kurisutaru* or *kurisutaru mesu.*
> **Ao-esu** (blue *S*). Speed pills.
> **Esu,** the letter *S,* short for *supiido,* "speed."
> **Kuranku,** "crank," as in "cranking up."
> **Rei** (cold). Methamphetamines.
> **Shabu.** Also *shabu shabu* and *tsumetai shabu shabu.* These words for methamphetamine are a pun on the Japanese dish *shabu shabu,* literally "swish-swish," in which sliced meat is dipped and stirred in boiling broth. The sound and action are similar to "cooking" methamphetamines.
> **Tsumetai mono.** Cold thing.

Much of the methamphetamines on Japan's streets today is manufactured outside the country, notably in North Korea. Smuggled into Japan, the drugs are sold on the streets by the *pombai,* the amphetamine dealers, also known as *shabuya,* "shabu shabu sellers," and *osuhito* or *oshinin,* "pushing man," a direct translation of the English term "pusher."

The newest drug dealers, who sell on the Internet, are called *nettopussha,* "net pushers."

> *Omae ni ii pombai shōkai shite yaru ze!*
> I'll introduce you to a cool speed-dealer!
> *Kono hen no atarashii pombai dare da? Ken ka?*
> Who's the new speed-dealer around here? Ken?

The meth junkie is known on Japan's streets as *ponchū* (from *hiropon chūdoku,* "methamphetamine-addicted"). Collectively they are called *ponchū zoku,* the "meth-addict gang." Other drug-jargon words for addict are *kyaku,* "guest" *kya,* for short. Those who use meth only occasionally are known as *tamapon,* from *tama* (occasional) and *ponchū.*

> *Oi! Ano ponchū shinisō ja nē ka.*
> Man, that meth freak looks like he's on his way out.
> *Ano ponchū mikka nete nē no ni, mada gin gin da ze!*
> That meth freak hasn't slept for three days, and he's still going strong!

Illicit safe-houses or "amp pads," known as *ponkutsu,* "amphetamine caverns," have sprung up nationwide. Here addicts buy, sell, and indulge their addiction in a relatively safe, clublike atmosphere. These are also called *kusurihako,* "medicine cabinet."

> *Omē no ponkutsu, ikura gurai da yo?*
> What are the prices like at your a-pad?
> *Moto yaoya datta no o aitsu-ra ponkutsu ni shita!*
> It used to be a grocery, but they turned it into an a-pad!

(HOMO. Gay.)

Homo and *gei* (gay) are direct borrowings from English: *gei* is a more recent arrival on the Japanese scene than *homo,* and is considered a more trendy expression. "*Aitsu gei?*" (He's gay?) is more neutral than the slightly more aggressive "*Aitsu homo?*"

(He's a homo?), but both words can be used in compounds interchangeably, with *gei* being the more acceptable choice.

> **Gei aniki** (gay older brother). A masculine homosexual.
> **Gei bideo.** Gay video or DVD. Also *gei bide*.
> **Gei burogu.** Gay blog.
> **Gei dōga.** Gay movie. Also *gei mūbii*.
> **Gei kurabu.** Gay club or bar. Also *gei bā*.
> **Gei manga.** Gay manga comics.
> **Gei matcho.** Macho gay.
> **Gei mikkusu** (gay mix). An evening at a club with a mixed gay and straight crowd.
> **Gei naito.** Gay night at a club.
> **Gei pātei.** Gay party.
> **Gei poruno komiku.** Gay-porn comics.
> **Gei purofairu.** Gay profile (on a website).
> **Gei saito.** Gay website.
> **Gei sauna.** Gay sauna.
> **Gei sefure** (gay sex-friend). Someone met regularly for sex only; a "fuck buddy."
> **Gei shoppu.** Gay store selling goods to a predominantly gay and lesbian clientele.
> **Gei shōsetsu.** Gay novel.
> **Gei zasshi.** Gay magazine or journal.

The popular expression *gei bōi*, however, is not a "gay boy" in the American sense of the word, nor is the boy necessarily young or gay; a *gei bōi* or a *gei-bōi-san*, a "Mr. Gay Boy," is a man affecting effeminate airs—*hoge hoge*, in gay slang—who works in a gay club (more often than not in drag), serving and entertaining customers, regardless of his sexual preference. Those who work exclusively in drag are also called *misutā redei* (Mr. Lady), and *josoko*, "female clothing child."

> **Ken wa okama ja nai kedo, shigoto de gei bōi to shite hataraite'run da.**
> Ken's not really a queer, he just works at a drag bar.

> *Chotto, ano gei bōi sannin yonde kurenai? Ato, sham-*
> *pen mo ne!*
> Waiter, send those three "girls" over here? And some
> champagne!
> *Oi! Ano gei-bōi-san no kite'ru doresu mita ka yo? Zen*
> *zen sensu nai!*
> Hey, did you see the dress on that queen? No taste!

Clubs will have signs saying:

> *Gei-bōi-san-tachi to enjyoi shite kudasai.*
> Please enjoy yourself with the Mr. Gay Boys.
> *Nihonjin dake no gei-bōi-san de ganbatte orimasu.*
> Only Japanese Mr. Gay Boys do their best [at entertaining
> customers] at this club.

In some compounds, *homo* is more common than *gei*. *Homo anime* is used more than *gei anime*, for anime with gay erotic or pornographic content. *Homo bā* is used quite often for a gay bar, particularly among gay cliques. *Homogari*—a word made up of *homo* and *kari* (hunting)—means "gay bashing." *Geigari* is also used, but rarely. *Gei oyaji* (gay dad), an older gay man, is not as popular as *homo-oyaji*, which is usually used as a positive expression by those preferring older men. *Homo-ossan* (homo uncle), on the other hand, is a negative word for a homosexual man who is considered past his prime.

A *yōshokuhomo*, a farmed homo—"farmed" as in "farmed salmon"—is a straight man who, because of the persistence of a gay friend, occasionally agrees to homosexual activity. Also straight is the *homo-uke* (homo popular), who, to his chagrin, is considered far more attractive by the gay crowd than by women.

In recent slang, *homochikku* (homo-tic) and *geichikku* (gay-tic) help point the finger at men who seem to be cultivating a feminine air. These are saucy concoctions inspired by the "-ic" ending of words such as "erotic" (*erochikku*). Two new gay slang-words for someone who is without a doubt homosexual are *ikahomo* and *ikanimo,* from *ika ni mo homosekkushuaru,* a "homosexual indeed."

> **Homochikku na yatsu.**
> A faggoty dude.
> **Sonna geichikku na hanashi yamero yo!**
> Stop talking like such a queen!
> **Geichikku na gurasan.**
> Gayish sunglasses.

A particularly handsome gay guy is called an *ikemen gei* or a *kakomen gei.* A tough-looking homosexual, and men who are into leather and bondage with other men, are referred to in Japan as *hādogei,* "hard gay," or *hādokoa,* "hard-core," which is short for *hādokoa gei,* "hard-core gay."

> **Ne, ne! Mite mite, onē-chan! Ano ikemen gei wa oishisō nē!**
> Ooh, girl, look, look! That hot one's cute!
> **Ano hādogei dare? Omae no kareshi?**
> Who's that hard-core dude? Your boyfriend?
> **Ano hādokoa no kusari omosō nē.**
> The chains on that leather queen look real heavy.
> **Ano futari no hādokoa, ittai dotchi ga dotchi de yaru'n darō?**
> Those two hard-core guys, I wonder who fucks who?

The term *hādogei* became a widely understood word throughout Japan after 2002, when the (straight) pro wrestler and comedian, Masaki Sumitani, began a series of comedy skits in which the character he portrayed, Razor Ramon Hard Gay, accosted bystanders while dressed in leather microshorts, leather cap, and chains, performing acts of charity while embarrassing his victims (often children) with provocative pelvic thrusts and comedic yelps and taunts. Bondage and leather fashion associated with the "Hard Gay" look is also popular in Japan among young straight men, who might identify themselves as *hādogei*, despite their heterosexuality.

Two rough words from Japanese prison slang are *anko*, for the man who takes on a passive homosexual role, and *kappa*, for the aggressive, active partner. Some say that the etymology for *anko* comes from a homonym dialect word meaning "maiden" or "young woman"; others believe that the word is inspired by the *anko* fish, a type of sea devil or monkfish that gulps and takes in anything that comes in its path. *Kappa* is a dangerous water sprite inhabiting ponds and rivers who attacks people's anuses.

In gay circles, boys and men who are definitely not gay are termed *nonke*, an amalgam of *non* and *ke* (feeling).

> **Watashi nonke ni shika kyōmi nai no.**
> Me, I prefer straight boys.
> **Yappari nonke!**
> So he's straight after all!
> **Nande aitsu omae to neta'n darō? Aitsu nonke ja nakatta?**
> How come he slept with you? I thought he was straight?

Nonke has developed into various new expressions used primarily for and about the *nonkesen* (nongay specializing), who are gay men mainly interested in sexual activity with straight men:

> **Kuware nonke** (gobbled nongay). A straight man who agrees to being fellated.
> **Nonke bā** (nongay bar). Bars for straight customers who enjoy watching gay floor shows.
> **Nonke Ei Bui** (nongay adult video). "Straight bait" pornography, a genre of DVDs and Internet feeds for a gay target audience, which show straight men involved in solo or gay activity.

Nonke hattenba (nongay development places). Cruising spots (*hattenba*) where gay men are likely to pick up straight men.

Nonke ikemen (nongay cool face). A straight hunk.

Nonke keijiban (nongay bulletin board). Internet forums and websites with tips and information on new DVDs, links, and information about hooking up with available straight men.

Nonke supōtsuman (nongay sportsman). The straight athlete type.

Nonke tōsan (nongay dad). Handsome, older straight men who might be available for gay sex.

Nonke-chan. A straight young man. A straight twink.

Nonke esu enu esu (nongay *SNS*). Nongay social network service.

Nonke-roshutsu (nongay exposure). Gay men exposing themselves to unsuspecting straight men.

(IKETERU! Cool!)

Every generation introduces its own favorite expressions for the word "good." What was "groovy" and "neat" many years ago in America became "cool" and "way to go," followed in the late 1980s by "awesome" and "rad." Then there was "kowabonga." There was "chill," there was "wicked," and then finally in the 2000s a retro reinstitution of "awesome," "cool," "sweet"—and a group of zany new terms like "off the hizzle."

In Japan as well, each new generation discards the previous generation's appreciative exclamations and then institutes its own, sometimes cringing at what was cool a generation ago, and other times rediscovering older expressions.

Anyone connected to Japan's cool crowd today will try to avoid the following exclamations:

Ikasu (to cause to go) is parallel to "swell" or "neat" in America. *Ikasu* was followed by *kimatte'ru,* which today might still be used by an aging groovy aunt, but no one else. *Nau da!* was the rage of the 70s, literally meaning "It is now!" This was followed by *nauii,* an inspired transformation of "now" into an adjectival "now-y," meaning "trendy" or "groovy." People will cringe, but also laugh, if you call anything *nauii.*

The late 70s and early 80s saw *kakkoii,* which hatched from the phrase *kakko no ii* (well-shaped, good-looking), and the early nineties brought *Sugē gū!* (Totally good!); *Mechanko gū!* (Messed-up good!); and *Mechakucha gū!* (Fucked-up good!).

So what is awesome, cool, or off the hizzle now in the Japan of the 2010s?

Kakkoii from the late 1980s has returned, and is being used by everyone from teenagers to the *arafuifu* (fifty-somethings—a contraction of the English phrase "around fifty").

Reigning supreme in 2010 is *Iketeru!* (Awesome!), which became the predominant cool word when the prime-time Fuji TV Saturday program *Mechamecha Iketeru!* began in 1996. This very popular show from the Kansai area, with its zany expressions, has had a significant linguistic effect on young Japan. Both the program and *iketeru* have remained favorites for the past fifteen years.

An even newer form of *iketeru*, which should not be used by anyone nearing twenty-five, is *ike-ike*. Its adjective is *ike-ike na* (though sometimes in the excitement the *na* is dropped).

> **Ike-ike na hito.** An ace guy.
> **Ike-ike na saito.** A, like, awesome site.
> **Ike-ike na ikemen.** A mega-hot guy. (*Ikemen*, "hunk," is itself made up of *ike*, "cool," and *men*, "face.")

Another interesting phenomenon are the neologisms of Shoko Nakagawa, a major idol, actress, and energetic blogger. She has introduced her own personal variations of "awesome," and her words have caught on. Since she began her Shokotan blog in 2004—currently the single most influential blog in Japan, with over a billion hits—she has introduced a string of terms that are used throughout the country. These neologisms are in fact called *shokotan-go*, "Shokotan words": *giza*, for instance, means "totally" or "very." An even stronger "very" is *giganto* (giant); stronger still is *gigantikku* (gigantic); and even stronger *bigguban* (big bang). These can be used like the American intensifiers "mega," "awesome," "wicked."

> **Giza ii!** Mega-good.
> **Giza oishi!** Mega-tasty, or mega-cute.
> **Giganto ii!** Wicked good.
> **Giganto oishi!** Wicked cute.
> **Bigguban ii! Bigguban oishi!** Off-the-radar good and cute.

In her blog, Shoko Nakagawa has even appropriated *kakkoii*, the longest-living Japanese trend-word for "cool," and turned it into *kakoyosu*.

(IMO. Hick.)

For generations *imo*, the potato, has been a symbol of the hick in Japan. Any Japanese not born or at least raised in Tokyo or in another of the metropolises could qualify in urban slang as an *imo*. In the past decade the potato, in its scorn of out of towners, has acquired new dimensions.

> **Gee! Ano imo sugē kakkō shite'ru!**
> Man! I can't believe what that hick's wearing!
> **Nani shabette'n no ka waka'nnai yo, ano imo!**
> I don't understand a word this bumpkin's saying!

Even more offensive than *imo* is *imo yarō*, "potato guy."

> **Ano imo yarō jibun no koto kakkoii to omotte'n no!**
> **Tondemonē!**
> This geek thinks he's cool! Well, I got news for him!

To be cruel to out-of-town girls, the term *imo nē-chan*, "potato sister," was invented.

> **Ore warui kedo! Anna imo nē-chan to dēto shinē yo!**
> Sorry, man! No way I'm gonna go on a date with a yokel like her!

Potato terms originating in Tokyo's schools are *potēto* itself and *imozoku,* "potato gang."

> ***Ano potēto ota ota ota ota shichatte, shōganai na! Tōkyō ni narete nai kara na!***
> I'm not surprised that poor hick's freaking out! He's not used to Tokyo!
> ***Ore Tōkyō ni kaeritē yo! Kono hen no yatsu-ra minna imozoku nan da mon!***
> I wanna go back to Tokyo! This dump's fulla hicks!

Other *imo*-related insults on the slang scene are *korokke,* "potato croquettes," and *imochi* (an abbreviated version of *imo chippusu*), "potato chips."

> ***Oi! Korokke! Dok'kara kita'n da yo!***
> Man, what a boob! What stone did you crawl out from under?
> ***Asoko ni atsumatte'n no wa minna imochi!***
> The dudes who hang out there are a bunch of hicks!

If a person from the provinces is a "potato," a "croquette," or a "chip," then his actions or style could be labeled "potatoesque," "croquette-ish," or "chiplike." The endings *-kusai, -ppok,* and *-chikku* (from the "-tic" in romantic) can be added to any of the above nouns to turn them into adjectives such as *imokusai, imoppoi, imochikku,* or *potētochikku.*

> ***Aa! Mō! Uchi no okā-san imoksai! Issho ni dearukitaku-nai yo!***
> God! My mother's such a hick! I can't stand to be seen with her!
> ***Ano ko no apāto'tte, chō-imoppoi!***
> That girl's apartment's just so tacky!

Imochikku hanasanaide yo! Kikoeru ja nai!
Don't talk like a hillbilly! People will hear!
Atashi kare to disuko ni itte mo, potētochikku odoru kara 'ya na no!
I don't wanna be seen in a club with him! He dances like some hick!

(JITO JITO. Wet.)

There is a group of words fashionable on the street for discussing a vagina's degree of wetness during sexual arousal. Even though these lively words evoke splashy and watery sounds, they belong to the more profane expressions in the Japanese language.

The standard verb meaning "to get wet" is *nureteru*, which can be used in reference to female sexual arousal:

> ***Kanojo no asoko nureteru.***
> Her pussy's getting wet.
> ***Kare no koto kangaeta dake de, atashi mō nureru!***
> All I have to do is think about him and I get wet!

Nureteru inspired the slightly nastier *nuru nuru*. In the geometric progression of wetness, *nuru nuru* implies the first manifestations of sexual interest, and consequently is a regular on pornographic DVD titles.

> ***Ore itsumo kanojo no asoko nuru nuru ni suru tame ni yubi de ijikuru'n da.***
> To get her snatch moist, I always finger it a bit.
> ***Ore ga heya ni haite iku dake de, kanojo no asoko wa nuru nuru ni naru'n da!***
> All I have to do is walk into the room, and her pussy gets moist!

> **Mō atashi nuru nuru nan dakara, hayaku chōdai yo!**
> I'm already moist, baby—give it to me, quick!

The next step up on the ladder of profanity brings us to *jito jito* and *jittori*. When this is used to discuss a vagina, the implication is that it is definitely ready for intercourse.

> **Aang! Atashi no asoko jittori nurete kichatta mitai!**
> Ooh! My pussy's getting all hot and juicy!
> **Atashi no asoko ga jito jito shinai'n dattara, kuriimu o tsukau wa.**
> If my pussy doesn't get wet, I just use some cream.

Next in line are *bicho bicho, becho becho,* and *bisho bisho*. These are used to avow that the vagina has become very wet indeed. The successful DVD series *Nure Nure Bichoman* (Moist Moist Drenched-Cunt) has also made *bichoman* (drenched cunt) a popular term.

> **Ore honto ni kanojo no asoko o kawaigatta kara, don don bicho bicho ni natta!**
> I fondled her snatch till she was wet and willing!
> **Atarashiku katta baibu, sore sugokute sa! Mō san-pun gurai de asoko bicho bicho ni natchau yo!**
> That new dildo I bought is fuckin' great! In like three minutes my pussy's all wet!
> **Kanojo wa ore ni sugē kureijii da yo! Datte kanojo no asoko wa itsumo becho becho da mon!**
> I can tell she's nuts for me the way her pussy's always juicy!
> **Atashi sugoi kōfun shiteta no ni, nanka becho becho ni wa naranakatta'n da yo ne!**
> Even though I was real turned-on, for some reason I wasn't getting wet!
> **Ore kanojo no sugē bisho bisho ni natta asoko ni buchikonda ze!**
> I plunged right into her wet snatch!

The final supertaboo *G* group is *gucho gucho, gusho gusho,* and *gusshori.* These imply that the woman is writhing in total ecstasy and that the orgasmic juices are positively gushing out.

The official term for vaginal secretion is *chikō*, written with the characters for "shame" and "dirt." In fact *chikō* refers to both male and female smegma, though *mankasu* (cunt dirt) and *chinkasu* (dick dirt) are the more common negative and gender-specific words. The more positive terms, in descending order of elegance, are *honkijiru* (truthful soup); *sekkusujiru* (sex soup); *erojiru* (erotic soup); *aieki* (love liquid); *rabujūsu* (the English term "love juice"); *manjiru, mankojiru,* and *omekojiru,* all meaning "cunt soup"; and, perhaps somewhat strangely, *sukebejiru* (lecher soup).

(KECHI. Stingy.)

Kechi originated during the early Edo period (1603–1868). It was initially pronounced *keshi*, and meant "shabby" or "dingy." Over time this term grew in currency. Recent trends have given *kechi* a feminine touch; many men avoid it as too cute.

> *Onegai otō-san! Kechi!*
> Oh come on, dad! You're so stingy!
> *Atashi anna kechi na otoko to zettai kekkon shinai wa.*
> I'm not gonna get married to such a stingy guy.
> *Kanojo wa kechi dakara zenzen asobi ni dekakenai!*
> She's so stingy she never goes anywhere!

To emphasize someone's tightfistedness you can use *kechi* twice, or add the popular Osaka-dialect *do-*.

> *Kechikechi suru.*
> He's a gripe.
> *Kechikechi shinaide!*
> Don't be so stingy!
> *Dokechi dakara mō issho ni dekakenai!*
> He's so tightfisted I'm not going out with him anymore!

Other variations on *kechi* are *kechikusai* (looking or acting stingy), or *kechimbō*, "cheapskate" or "tightwad."

> **Dōshite sonna ni kechikusai?**
> Why're you so cheap?
> **Ano kechimbō no jiji nani itta'n da?**
> What did that old cheapskate tell you?

Another handy synonym for *kechi* is *sekoi*, "stingy."

> **Bōifurendo sekokute, tanjobi purezento kurenai no.**
> My boyfriend's so stingy, I don't get birthday presents.

A stronger, more masculine variation on parsimony is *gametsui*, popular in the Osaka dialect. It is thought that this word comes from *kame*, "turtle," and *tsui*, from *tsuku*, "to cling"—the idea being that turtles stubbornly cling to whatever they bite.

> **Ano gametsui onna-me ore ni kane kaese'tte ii yagaru!**
> That cheap bitch told me to give her her money back!
> **Nan de sonna ni gametsui'n da yo?**
> Why are you such a cheapskate?

To emphasize greed and the element of hoarding, you can use *gatsu gatsu*. (For maximum effect, say *gatsu gatsu gatsu gatsu* in quick succession.)

> **Kanojo wa itsumo ie ni ite, gatsu gatsu kane o tamete'ru.**
> She's always home hoarding her money.
> **Uchi no bā-san nannen mo gatsu gatsu gatsu gatsu takuwaete'ru kara ima ja okuman chōja da yo!**
> Grandma's been hoarding cash for years now! She must be a multimillionaire by now!

(KEIMUSHO. Prison.)

The word *keimusho* is made up of three characters: *kei*, "punishment"; *mu*, "duty"; and *sho*, "place." It became the official word for prison at the end of the Taisho period (1912–26), replacing the older *kangoku* (*kan*, "supervise," plus *goku*, "jail"). Today both words are used colloquially.

> ***Ore wa Abashiri ni itta ze! Asoko wa sekai ichi hidē keimusho da!***
> I was in Abashiri! Man, the worst prison in the world!
> ***Omae dore gurai kangoku ni ittan da?***
> How long were you in the pen for?

Also popular are the detention centers, known as *kōchisho.*

> ***Aitsu ga kōchisho ni iku no wa hajimete ja nai kara nā!***
> It's not the first time he's ended up in the slammer!
> ***Ore wa ano kōchisho de wa hidē me ni atta zo.***
> I had a fucking hard time in that lockup.

Imprisonment or confinement is officially called *kankin,* the character *kan* meaning "supervision," and *kin*, "prohibition." Some useful phrases to remember are:

> ***Kankin suru.*** To imprison.
> ***Kankin sareru.*** To be put in prison.
> ***Kankin saseru.*** To get someone put in prison.

Even though *kankin* is the official word for incarceration, it is as familiar in the streets as in the courtroom.

> ***Damare! Omae ore ga kankin sarete mō ii no ka yo?***
> Shut up! You wanna get me arrested?
> ***Ore hayaku koko denakya! Kankin sarechimau yo!***
> I've got to get the hell outta here! They're gonna arrest me!

The first place one lands after being arrested is the *butabako* (pig-box), which is the lockup at every local police station.

A *butabako* is usually a small room with a wooden floor that is shared by up to five or six suspects awaiting arraignment. A popular street-slang variation on *butabako* is *torikago,* "birdcage," and *ambako,* "dark box," which can be used for both police cells and prison cells.

> *Aitsu satsu o uchisokonete butabako ni itchimatta.*
> He shot at a policeman, so they put him in the clink.
> *Ano torikago wa abunē tokoro da.*
> That birdcage's a dangerous place.
> *Baka yarō! Koko wa ambako da ze! Onsen ryokō* ja nēnda!*
> Get your ass in gear! This is a lockup, not Club Med!
> *Ano ambako ni ichido haittara, tada ja derenē.*
> Once you're in that slammer, you don't get out so easy.

One of the more popular words for jail in rough street speech is *musho,* the last two syllables of *keimusho.*

> *Kawaisō ni, anta no danna mata musho iki datte sā.*
> Your poor old man! So he's inside again.
> *Mata aitsu-ra ga kore no koto kagitsuketara, ore mata musho iki darō na!*
> If they find me with this stuff on me, I'll end up in the clink again!

Three tongue-in-cheek street euphemisms for jail are *hoteru,* "hotel"; its inversion *teruho;* and the elegant *bessō,* "villa" or "holiday home."

> *Uchi no teishu sengetsu mata hoteru ni haitchatta!*
> Last month my old man checked into the Crossbar Hotel again!

---

*Literally, a "hot-spring trip."

> ***Ore ga kono teruho kara derareru nante maru de ten-***
> ***goku da ze!***
> I'll be in fucking heaven once I'm out of the Big House.
> ***Ato ichinen de teruho kara derareru!***
> I'm gonna be outta this resort in a year!
> ***Omē no nyōbō wa doko no bessō ni iru'n da?***
> What villa are they keeping your old woman at?
> ***Sonna koto shitara bessō iki da.***
> If you do such things, you'll end up at the villa.

Entering prison is unofficially known as *inkyo*, "retire-ment." Being imprisoned is referred to as *heinonaka*, "within walls." The time or the term that a prisoner serves is known as *keiki*, "punishment period," and in criminal slang as *otsutome*, "duty," especially in Yakuza circles, where it is seen as the "duty" of subordinates to do prison terms in place of their bosses. *Nagamushi* (its somewhat cryptic etymology is "long six-four") means "a long prison term," and *shombenkei*, "piss term," is a shorter sentence.

> ***Ore no tsuma mata inkyo shita.***
> My old woman's inside again.
> ***Aitsu wa inkyo suru no mo sandome da nā.***
> This is the third time he's inside.
> ***Aitsu otsutomechū!***
> He's serving time!
> ***Ore no otsutome mo ato ni nen de oshimai da.***
> My term's gonna be over in two years.

The most important word for the Japanese inmate, the light at the end of the dark tunnel, is *shaba*, the "outside world." *Shaba* originated in India as the Sanskrit *saha*, meaning the "world we live in." It came to Japan in the sixth century B.C.E. with the advent of Buddhism, and over the centuries has been absorbed into colloquial speech in such expressions as *Mō shaba ni yō wa nai!* (I have no more use for this world!).

> **Shaba e deru.**
> To leave prison.
> **Shaba ni dete koreta kimochi wa dō da?**
> How does it feel now that you're out?

Inmates impatient to get their share of *shaba* before they are legally eligible might try breaking jail, known as *yaburu* (break), or *retsuwaru*, which is criminal jargon for breaking out with an accomplice (*retsu* is the inversion of *tsure*, "together," and *waru* means "break").

> **Ore wa yaburu keikaku ga aru.**
> I've got a plan to get outta here.
> **Omē ikkai haitchimattara, yaburu hōhō nante nē zo.**
> Once you're in there, man, there's no way of escape.
> **Ken to Toshi wa mō retsuwatta.**
> Ken and Toshi broke out of jail.
> **Ore-tachi ni wa retsuwaru shika nēn da!**
> We're gonna have to beat this joint!

A jailbreaker is called *usagi*, "rabbit," while a fugitive who manages to leave Japan is known as *takatobi*, "high flier."

(KETSU. Ass.)

The *proper* word for posterior in Japanese is *dembu*, but like its English equivalent, its popularity rating in street slang is low. In situations where Americans say "bottom" or "ass," the Japanese words to use are *shiri* or the slightly rougher *ketsu*.

> **Unko o shita ato ketsu o fuku.**
> You wipe your ass after you shit.
> **Kondo watashi ga hirotta otoko wa ōkii na kebukai ketsu no otoko yo!**
> The guy I picked up the other day was big and hairy-assed!

> *Kanojo wa itsumo ketsu o furimawashite aruite, maru*
> *de kyabasuke da na.*
> She always wiggles her ass like that when she walks. What
> a slut.
> *Eēē? Anta no danna'tte anta no ketsu ni yaritai'tte?*
> *Sonna no ammari da yo ne. Dō sun'no?*
> What? Your husband wants to do it from behind? That's
> terrible! What're you gonna do?

Ketsu is written with the same character as *ana*, which
means "hole." But to specify the anus, *ketsu no ana*, or "asshole," is used.

> *Ketsu no ana de yatta koto aru?*
> You ever fucked anyone up the ass?
> *Ketsu no ana no chiisai yarō!*
> You cheap asshole! (Literally, "Your asshole is small!")
> *Ore ketsu no ana ga okashii mitai da. Nanka itē'n da yo.*
> Something's wrong with my hole. It kinda hurts.

Ketsuware means "ass crack," and a slangy term for jock-
strap is *ketsuwaresapōta*, "ass-crack supporter," *ketsuwaresapō*
for short.

The other important word for ass is *shiri*, "bottom." *Shiri*
is softer than *ketsu*, which makes it the preferred word among
women.

> *Kono kuriimu shiri ni nureba yoku narimasu.*
> If you rub this cream on your bottom, it'll get better.
> *Nan da! Omae sonna dekai shiri shite, sonna jii-pan*
> *hakeru to omotteru no ka?*
> With a fat ass like yours, you expect to get into jeans like
> those? Please!
> *Omae no shiri kusai!*
> Your ass stinks!

People discussing bottoms in public will usually add the softening honorific prefix *o-* to *shiri.*

> *Atashi oshiri ga itai'n da, iboji ja nē ka to omou.*
> My bottom hurts—I hope it's not hemorrhoids!
> *Kare minna no iru mae de atashi no oshiri sawatto no!*
> He grabbed my bottom in front of everyone!
> *Anta sonna doresu katta'tte? Mariko no dekai oshiri ni dō yatte hakasen no yo?*
> You bought *that* dress? How's Mariko supposed to get her fat ass into it?

Many proverbs involving bottoms are socially acceptable. If, for instance, you wish to imply that someone is wasting time, you could say that this person's efforts are *Shiri ni megusuri*— "Putting eyedrops in his or her bottom." To imply that you or someone else has to leave posthaste, you could use *Shiri ni ho kakeru*—"Tying a sail to one's bottom." If people laugh at weaknesses that they themselves might be guilty of, you could say, *Saru no shiri warai*—"One monkey laughing at another monkey's ass." To comment upon a culprit whose guilt will sooner or later surface, you could quote this ostrich proverb: *Atama kakushite shiri kakusazu*—"You may hide your head, but your ass will show."

Crasser words that have gained popularity on the streets, like *ketsumedo, shippe,* or *shippeta,* started off as regional dialect words. *Ketsumedo* is a combination of *ketsu* and the Kansai dialect word *medo,* which literally means "aim" or "object." *Shippe* and *shippeta* originally came from the Niigata dialect, and specifically mean "buttocks" or "buns."

> *Ichinichijū suwatte'ru kara, ketsumedo ga taresagatchimatta.*
> My ass has dropped 'cause I sit all day.
> *Ore wa shippeta o pan pan tatakareru no ga suki da!*
> I love getting my ass spanked!

(KINTAMA. Balls.)

In Japan, a testicle is officially known as *kōgan*. The most popular word, however, favored by old and young nationwide, is *kintama*, "golden balls."

Kintama is one of the few ancient Japanese slang words that have thrived throughout the centuries. Although today it is written with the characters *kin*, "gold," and *tama*, "ball," this word began its venerable career as a fusion of the characters *ki*, meaning "life," and *tama*, meaning "soul."

> **Shinjirarenē! Kanojo ore no kintama sawatte'ta! Nante onna da!**
> Man, I couldn't believe it! She grabbed my balls! What a woman!
> **Gee! Ano otoko hitomae de jibun no kintama kakimushitte'ru no mita ka yo?**
> Yuck! Did you see that man scratch his balls in front of everyone?

Another popular expression for testicles is *tama*, literally "balls." (Be careful, however; in some dialects it means "penis.")

> **Aa! Tama ga kayui nā!**
> Man! My balls itch!
> **Mizugi no waki kara tama ga miechatta!**
> I saw his balls hanging out from under his trunks!

If you need to discuss testicles in mixed company or in refined surroundings, the word to choose would be *kyūsho*. It is made up of the characters *kyū*, meaning "critical" or "crucial," and *sho*, meaning "place." As this particular expression accentuates the susceptibility of a testicle, it is favored by sports announcers and the like on those occasions when a ball inadvertently incapacitates a player during baseball, golf, or other dangerous sports.

> *Kore wa bōru ga kyūsho ni atatta yō desu ne! Itai desu ne!*
> Ooh! That ball hit him in a vulnerable spot! That must hurt!
> *Atashi kuruma no doa aketara, kare no chōdo kyūsho ni atatchatte sā! Kare 'ttara shinisō datta yo!*
> When I opened the car door, I hit him right in the balls! He looked like he was gonna die!

A streetwise proverb is *Teki no kyūsho wa waga kyūsho*, which means "My enemy's 'soft spot' is my 'soft spot.'" This proverb (which by the way is of Chinese origin) means that you are well prepared for a confrontation with your opponent, as you know that his weak points are the same as yours.

Two cruder street-favorites for testicle are *oinari-san* and *oinaribukuro*. *Oinari-san* is a type of sushi that originated in Osaka and looks remarkably like balls. *Oinaribukuro* is a variation of this idea, *bukuro*, "sack," referring to the roundish sack of deep-fried tofu (*abura age*) in which the vinegared sushi rice is stuffed.

> *Furo ga sugē atsusugite, ore nanka oinari-san yakedo suru ka to omotta!*
> The bath was so hot I thought I was gonna burn my balls!
> *Atashi, sā, kare no kemukujara no oinaribukuro ga momo ni ataru no ga suki na no.*
> I love it when his hairy balls rub against my thigh.

(KURO. Opium.)

The most popular word for opium on the Japanese streets is *kuro*, literally "black," a name inspired by the black, tarry texture of the drug.

> *Ore kono kuro mita dake de hai ni natchimau yo!*
> Man, I get high just by looking at that shit!
> *Ittai ore-tachi kono kuro utte, ikura kasegeru to omou?*
> How much do you think we'll make selling this black?

The actual word for opium is *ahen*. It is made up of the characters *a*, for "pleasure" or "delectation," and *hen*, meaning a "morsel": a morsel of happiness. Throughout Japan's history, this "morsel" has cost many citizens their heads. Opium was the first forbidden drug in Japan. It initially appeared during the Muromachi period (1333–1573), in the fourteenth century, and was used for medicinal purposes. By the Edo period (1603–1868), recreational use of opium had become so popular that the authorities clamped down with the death penalty. Even to-day, laws in Japan are strict compared to the West.

> *Kono ahen dō surun da yo? Sū no ka?*
> What're you gonna do with that opium? You gonna smoke it?
> *Wakaru darō? Kono iro to nioi! Kono ahen wa besuto da ze!*
> You can tell, man! The color, the smell—this opium's top grade!

Other casual references to opium are *nama*, "raw," and *yāpin*, the Japanese pronunciation of the Chinese word for opium, *yapian*.

> *Kono nama, marifana to mikusu shite miru yo. Sugoi ze!*
> Try mixing that opium with marijuana. It's great, man!
> *Kono yāpin wa Hon Kon san da.*
> This opium's from Hong Kong

Another popular word for opium is *tsugaru*. It refers to the domestic raw opium, brown like coffee grounds, that is grown illicitly on the plains of Tsugaru, a fertile region of northern Japan.

> *Nani? Kore ga tsugaru da'tte? Iro ga hen ja nai ka?*
> What? This stuff's Tsugaru opium? Ain't the color weird?
> *Tsugaru ichikiro katchimaō ze! Sore de shōbai dekiru yo!*
> Let's get a whole kilo of this Tsugaru stuff! We can make a bundle!

Opium eaters are generally known formally as *ahen jōyōsha.* Favorite street words for "opium eater" are *ahenchū, kurochū,* or *namachū (chū* is short for *chūdoku,* "addiction").

> **Atarimae da yo! Aitsu wa ahenchū sā! Me o mireba, sugu wakaru!**
> Of course he's an opium addict! Look at his eyes, you can tell!
> **Ore-tachi kono hen no kurochū ni kore ureru ze.**
> Let's unload this stuff on the opium freaks around here.
> **Anta ano namachū wa sugokatta yo! Buru buru furue-te'n da mon!**
> Man, you should have seen that opium freak! He was like shaking all over!

Safe houses and clubs that act as "opium dens" are officially known as *ahen kyūinjo,* or more popularly as *ahen kutsu,* "opium den," or *kuro kutsu,* "black den."

> **Shitte'ru ka, ano Roppongi no kurabu? Ima wa mō ahen kutsu ni natta.**
> You know that club in Roppongi? It's turned into an opium den.
> **Nimotsu matomete koko dero yo! Koko wa kuro kutsu ja nēn da!**
> Pack your bags and get outta here! This isn't an opium den!

(MANZURI. Female masturbation.)

An interesting fact worth noting is that although American slang can boast of an overwhelming assemblage of words for male masturbation, it seems to have few slang terms for female masturbation beyond "frig" and "diddle." In the case of masturbation, Japanese slang is much more gender-equal—male and female masturbation are each represented by a rich bouquet of slang words.

Manzuri, literally "ten thousand rubs," is the most common of this group, and is related to the colloquial Japanese word for male masturbation, *senzuri,* "a thousand rubs." *Manzuri suru* or *manzuri yaru* are the most customary verb forms.

> *Ně! Honto ni manzuri shitara hada ga kirei ni naru no? Ichi nichi ni nankai shinakya dame?*
> Is it true that if you play with yourself it's good for your skin? How often a day are you supposed to do it?
> *Aa! Atashi manzuri ni wa aki aki da wa! Hommono no chimpoko hoshii yo!*
> I've had enough of playing with myself! I want some real dick!

Two other variations of *manzuri* are the closely related *omankosuri* ("cunt rub," also pronounced by some *omakosuri*) and its fashionable Osaka variation, *omekosuri.*

> ***Ano dibuidi sugē ze! Omankosuri yatte'n no marumie***
> ***nan da mon!***
> That DVD's ace! This chick's giving it to herself and you can
> see everything!
> ***Atashi neru mae ni maiban kanarazu omekosuri yaru!***
> I always bang my box a little before I go to sleep at night!

In the same *omanko / omeko* group (these two words are
the most popular slang words for vagina in Japan) are the
expressions *temanko* and *temeko*, both meaning "hand-cunt,"
which are also used for male masturbation (the man's hand
taking the place of a vagina).

> ***Omē! Kanojo mechakucha temanko shita ze!***
> Yo man! She was really giving it to herself!
> ***Anta-ra futari sorotte temeko shita'tsū no? Honto ka yo?***
> Did you girls really finger-fuck each other? Are you serious?

Two other noteworthy words for "diddling" are *bobowaru*
and *nigiribobo*. The *bobo* in both words refers to the vagina, *bobo*
being a popular Kyushu-dialect slang word that has become a favorite throughout Japan. *Bobowaru* literally means "splitting the
vagina"; *nigiribobo*, "grab-vagina," besides its primary allusion to
"diddling," can also mean forcing one's clenched hand through a
woman's clasped thighs in order to reach her vagina.

> ***Onna ga bobowaru no mita koto aru ka? Dō yaru'n darō?***
> Have you ever seen a woman play with herself? I wonder
> how they do it?
> ***Kanojo wa ireru mae kanarazu ore ni nigiribobo saseru.***
> She always lets me fondle her snatch a bit before I put it in.

Two expressions favored in sex-business circles are *yubi
ningyō*, "finger doll," and *yubizeme*, "finger attack." (*Ningyō*,

"doll," is a euphemism for dildo.) *Yubizeme* has a broad range of meaning, especially in the jargons of Soapland massage parlors. If, for instance, the customer pays extra, the *sōpujo*, "soap girl," will do what is also termed *yubizeme*, "finger attack," on his anus, which involves in-depth manipulation and finger penetration. By association, *yubizeme* can also be used of a customer "finger attacking" the soap girl.

> ***Chotto yubi ningyō suru no wa ii yo.***
> A bit of fingering doesn't do any harm.
> ***Atashi yubizeme de shika ikanai'n no! Bōifurendo tsukaenē yo!***
> I usually just play with myself! My boyfriend's useless!

Two "frig" words that originated in the rougher areas of Tokyo are the traditional *ateire*, "blocking and entering," and the foreign-inspired *suichi o ireru*, "flicking the switch," which could be translated into American slang as "fingering a clit."

> ***Atashi monogokoro tsuite kara zutto ateire shit'n no yo.***
> I've been finger-fucking myself ever since I can remember.
> ***Ano sutorippā wa ore no me no mammae de suitchi o irete yagatta.***
> That stripper was fingering her clit right in front of my face.

Slang speakers are always interested in new expressions to add to their repertoire. In the case of female masturbation, some of the strongest new words have been imported from the popular Osaka dialect. Two of the important X-rated Osaka words used throughout Japan are *irou* and *irau*.

> ***Shinjirareru? Jibun no asoko irau no ga suki'tte!***
> Would you believe this? She said she likes playing with her thing!

> *Jūsansai no koro tomodachi ga dō yatte irou no ka misete kuretan no yo.*
> When I was thirteen a friend showed me how to play with it.

Finally, there are a group of words that are somewhat more graphic in the sense that they focus on the hand action during masturbation, and comment on its intensity.

The first rung on the ladder of intensity is *ijiru*, "to finger."

> *Mainichi ijitter'u?*
> Do you play with yourself every day?

The next step up the ladder is *ijirimawasu*, "to finger all around."

> *Atashi odoroichatta! Ken no ijirimawashikata umai'n da mon! Futsū no otoko wa shiranai no ni sa!*
> I was surprised Ken was so good at playing with my twat! Guys usually have no idea!

A word closely related to *ijirimawasu*, but even stronger, is *ijirimakuru*, "fingering around and around."

> *Atashi itsu demo doko demo asoko o ijirimakutchau! Gaman dekinai no yo!*
> I've always got this urge to play with myself! I can't help it!

The strongest word in this progression, and the strongest "diddle" word in the Japanese language, is the explosive *ijirimakuri-mawasu*, a word of violent intensity that English, for all its resourcefulness, could never match. Loosely translated it would read: "fingering in, out, and all round like there's no tomorrow."

(MARIFANA. Marijuana.)

The two most common pronunciations of marijuana in Japanese are *marifana* or *marippana*. Cannabis has been native to Japan for centuries. It never occurred to anyone to smoke it, but it played an important role in the daily life of the indigenous Ainus, who used it to make the cloth of their colorful costumes.

Japan's *Taima Torishimari Hō* (Hemp Control Act) carries stringent penalties, which has largely driven marijuana usage underground.

"Doing" marijuana can be translated into Japanese as *marifana o sū* or *marifana o yaru*.

> ***Nē, marippana suttara chūdoku natchau ka na?***
> Do you become an addict if you smoke marijuana?
> ***Kare'tte heya de marifana yatte'n da yo.***
> He's up in his room smoking pot.

The official word for marijuana is *taima*, "hemp." Past generations generally avoided the word, but its increasing use in the media has helped rekindle its popularity among the younger generation.

> ***Kono taima yatte minai? Suge hai ni naru yo!***
> Wanna try this marijuana? You'll get real high!
> ***Suzuko ima taima sabaite'ru ze! Nyū Yōku ni kone ga aru rashii.***
> Suzuko's selling marijuana! It seems she's got a connection in New York.

A slangier synonym for *taima* and *marifana* is *yasai*, "vegetables." Also popular are *kusa*, "grass," and *happa*, "leaves." These words parallel the American slang expressions "grass" and "weed."

> ***Oi, omē! Kono kusa no nioi kaide miro yo! Kore wa zettai saikōkyūhin da ze!***
> Yo, man! Take a whiff of this grass! Top-grade stuff!
> ***Ano happa sugē tsuyokute, ore kura kura shita yo! Honto da ze!***
> That weed was *so* strong, I was like hallucinating! I'm serious!

Hashish is known as *hashishu* or *hashishi*, and due to its darker color, *choko*, from *chokorēto*, "chocolate." A secret code name is also "844," as one of the readings of the numbers is *ha-shi-shi*.

> ***Ii choko ja nai. Dok' kara mitsuketa no?***
> Great marijuana. Where did you find it?
> ***Choko yatta ato 'tte, mō hara ga hete hara ga hete shōganē yo nā.***
> After we smoked that weed, we got the strongest munchies.

An important marijuana-related verb is *maku*, "to roll," as in "rolling a joint." By extension, a joint is called *rōru*, a "roll."

> ***Happa makeru dake nokotte'ru ka na?***
> Do we have enough grass to roll a joint?
> ***Happa no makikata shitte'ru?***
> You know how to roll a joint?

Another popular way of referring to marijuana is by its country of origin, by adding the word *san*, or "product of," to the country's name. Three typical types of "grass" are *Hawai san*, "Hawaiian"; *Tai san*, "Thai"; and *Indo san*, "Indian."

> ***Indo san yatta koto aru? Sugē ii yo!***
> Ever done Indian grass? It's ace!
> ***Kinō Tai san yattara sugē buttonjimatta!***
> We did some Thai yesterday and got seriously fucked-up, man!

> *Hawai san no hō ga ore wa suki da nā.*
> Me, my favorite's the Hawaiian stuff.

The Japanese equivalent to the American "pothead" or "user" is *happachū*, "leaf addict"; *kusachū*, "grass addict"; or *happaboke*, "grass doter." The suffix *-boke* is usually reserved for victims of the harder drugs, especially amphetamines. Used in reference to someone who indulges in lighter stuff, it has a comical nuance.

> *Omē ichinichijū kore suttara happachū ni naru no wa atarimae da!*
> Of course if you smoke this all day you're gonna turn into a pothead!
> *Aitsu sonna ni kusachū de itai'n dattara, hott'okeba! Ore-tachi ni kankei nē kara!*
> If he wants to be a total pothead, let him! It's not our problem!
> *Aitsu happaboke da yo na.*
> This guy's a regular grass fiend.

(MUNE. Breasts.)

Mune refers to an unspecified region of the torso, from approximately the stomach area to the larynx. It occurs in many colloquial phrases, such as *mune ga doki doki suru*, "the heart throbs"; *mune ga warui* (literally, "the stomach is bad"), "to be sickened by something"; or *mune ga sawagu* (the chest clamors), "to be excited." Besides these everyday idioms, *mune* is used by the modern generation to mean "breasts" or "tits."

> *Kanojo no mune wa saikō da ze!*
> Her tits are first-class!

> *Ore saisho ni me ni tsuku no ga mune nan da yo na.*
> The first thing I look at are a woman's breasts.

A word that ranks with the most important colloquialisms for breasts is *oppai*. In text messaging and online chats, *oppai* is often transformed into a witty *O81*, which can be read as *O-pa-i*. Consequently, boys and young men requesting breast photos online will ask for *O81-shashin*, "O81 pics."

> *Anta atashi no oppai momitai? Ii wa yo!*
> Wanna feel my breasts? Go ahead!
> *Kanojo kagandara oppai marumie da yo!*
> When she bends over, you can see her breasts!

Ingo (hidden language or slang) has a habit of inverting words to make them incomprehensible to outsiders. *Oppai*, which in the Japanese hiragana syllabary is written as *o-tsu-pai*, was inverted to create *paiotsu*. *Paiotsu* has been taken up by the porn industry, and is now more widely known.

> *Ano onna no paiotsu beron beron ni tarete'ru yo!*
> That woman's bazookas are dangling all the way down!
> *Betsu no onna yonde koi! Koitsu no paiotsu ja monotarinē!*
> Get me another girl! This one's tits aren't big enough!

Two words created from *oppai* to specify very small breasts are the veteran street-word *pechapai*, "flat breast," and the newer *rēzunpai*, "raisin pie," a pun suggesting that the breast is so small it could be a raisin.

> *Undō shisugiru kara kanojo pechappai no kimatte'ru yo.*
> I'm not surprised she hasn't any boobs, with all the exercise she's doing.

> ***Dō yū imi da yo, rēzunpai nante! Anta no, nanka, koyubi
> no saki gurai ja nai yo!***
> How dare you call me flat when my pinky's bigger than
> your dick!

Other *oppai*-related words in street and sex-slang circles are:

> **Dekapai** (big breasts). *Deka* is an Osaka word for "large"
> that is used throughout Japan.
> **Gipai** (pseudo-breasts). Usually used for padded breasts,
> but also for breasts with implants. A synonym is *gasepai*,
> "fake breasts."
> **Hamipai** (jutting breast). A breast that is partially or fully
> sticking out of a bra or blouse.
> **Mechapai** (extreme breasts). Very large breasts.
> **Oppaiseijin.** Breast aficionado.
> **Paichira** (breast flash). When a woman intentionally or un-
> intentionally exposes one or both breasts (or part of them).
> **Paishame.** Short for *oppai shashin mēru*. Pictures of
> breasts sent out as e-mail attachments or with mobile
> phones.
> **Paizuri** (breast-urbation). A woman using her breasts to
> bring a man to climax.
> **Tarepai.** Sagging breasts.

Chichi is another important word for breasts. The Chinese
character for *chichi* carries the connotation of suckling or
breast-feeding.

> **Dekai / chiisai chichi.**
> Big / small tits.
> **Kanojo wa buraja o tsukenai kara, chichi ga yure
> makuru.**
> Her tits bounce around 'cause she's not wearing a bra.

A slang word for women with small breasts is *naichichi*, "no-breast," with its anglicized synonym *nochichi*.

> **Kawaii kedo . . . naichichi!**
> She's cute . . . but no tits!
> **Aitsu nani-sama da omotte'n da yo? Nochichi no kuse ni!**
> Who the hell does she think she is? She doesn't even have tits!

Small breasts in general are known as *hinyū*, "poor breasts," while attractive yet small breasts are called *binyū*, "delicate breasts." Men particularly attracted to such breasts are known as *hinyūsen* and *binyūsen*, with *sen* meaning "specialist." Big breasts, on the other hand, are known as *kyonyū*, and men who are obsessed with them are known as *kyonyūsen*.

(NAMA. Condomless.)

In Japan, condoms are the most widely used form of contraception. Using condoms was the common practice long before the West launched its safe-sex campaigns in the 1980s. As a result, sex au naturel is regarded as a special delicacy.

Nama, "raw," originated in the *akasen*, the "red-line" district, where the munificent client could request exclusive "raw" service, involving sex or fellatio without a condom.

> ***Atashi nama dewa shinai! Datte ninshin shitaku nai mon!***
> I'm not gonna do it without a condom! I don't wanna get pregnant!
> ***Nama de yarō ze! Ore chanto iku mae ni nuku kara yo!***
> Let's do it without a condom! I promise to pull out just before I come!

Also related to *nama*, "raw," is the more potent *junnama*, "pure raw," a word coined by the condomless-sex enthusiasts of the Soapland massage parlors and the sex clubs.

> ***Ore kane ōme ni haratta kara junnama yareta.***
> I paid a lot, so I got to do it without a condom.
> ***Kondōmu torina! Junnama de yarō!***
> Take the rubber off! We'll do it without!

The other favorite slang expression for no-condom sex, *zatōichi*, originated in a more unlikely quarter, a popular Japanese children's television series. Its story takes place in the good old samurai days, with Zatōichi, the kind but bellicose leading man, ever ready to rescue a damsel in distress. What makes Mr. Zatōichi an exemplary candidate for the allusion to condomless sex is the fact that his trademark is the unsheathed sword—ever ready for action.

> **Atashi baka dakara ninshin shichatta yo! Aitsu ni zatōichi sasechatta kara!**
> Idiot that I am, I got pregnant! I let him do it without a rubber!
> **Zatōichi shitai'tte? Ryōkin wa nibai yo!**
> You wanna do it without? It'll cost you double!

The most indelicate synonym for *nama* (raw) is *sumara*, "bare penis."

> **Atashi nan da to omotte'n da! Otokui-san dake sumara sasete yaru'n dakara!**
> What do you think I am! It's only special customers I let do it without a rubber!
> **Ore kyō dōshite mo sumara yaritē!**
> Man, I really wanna do it without the party hat today!

When it comes to fellatio in the red-light district, the norm would be *fera kabuse*, "fellatio-covered," or *surippu*, "slip," a punny contraction of *sukin-rippu sābisu*, "skin (condom) lip service." During these trying times, "uncovered" is classified as a very expensive *supesharu sābisu* (special service). Two of the favorite designations for this type of fellatio are *nama ensō*, "live performance," and *namajaku*. *Namajaku* is a contraction of the longer *nama shakuhachi*, and literally means "raw *shakuhachi* flute." The *shakuhachi* is a vertical flute that is blown like a clarinet, and for centuries it has been a favorite red-light metaphor for fellatio.

> ***Anta mō nama ensō yametara? Saikin ironna byōki aru jan.***
> Shouldn't you stop sucking guys off? There's all kinda diseases out there.
> ***Warui kedo, atashi namajaku yaranai! Hai kondōmu!***
> Sorry, I only suck dick if you wear a rubber! Here's one!

(NANI KEI GA SUKI?
What's your type?)

The Japanese have endless options when it comes to specifying this or that type of person. However picky you may be, Japanese slang can pinpoint your type of man or woman.

> ***Arafokei.*** The forty-something type; from *arafo*, short for the Japanese pronunciation of "around forty," *araundo fōtei.*
> ***Arasakei.*** The thirty-something type; from *ara-sa*, short for the Japanese pronunciation of "around thirty," *araundo sātei.*
> ***Bishonenkei.*** The pretty-boy type.
> ***Botterikei.*** The plump type.
> ***Buijuarukei*** (the visual type). The young man, gay or straight, who wears makeup, gaudy clothing, and has eccentric hairstyles inspired by Japanese glam rock.
> ***Busukei.*** The ugly type.
> ***Debukei.*** The fat type; also *D-kei*, pronounced *diikei.*
> ***Dosurori.*** Fat girls in frilly baby-doll outfits. A fusion of *dosukoi* (a sumo wrestling exclamation) and Lolita.
> ***Emukei*** (the *M* type). The masochistic man or woman in S-M circles.
> ***Esukei*** (the *S* type). The sadistic man or woman in S-M circles.

Gachimuchikei (the plump but muscular type). A neologism used in gay circles.

Gangurokei (the blackface type). A woman with a deep tan and bleached hair, a style popular in the early 2000s. Though initially this was a style adopted by girls in their late teens, many *ganguro* who are still cultivating the look are now in their thirties.

Gatenkei (the manual-laborer type). In gay circles, men who either are or look like construction workers or mechanics.

Janiizukei (the Johnny's type). The cute, boy-band look, of the type managed by the major Japanese talent agency, Johnny & Associates. Also *Janikei* (Johnny type).

Kinnikukei. The muscular type.

Kogyarukei (the little girl type). Young women, usually fresh out of their teens, who are trend conscious and enjoy the company and attentions of maturer men.

Kumakei (bear type). The large, hairy man.

Makimaki-matchokei. The brawny, macho type.

Mamarorikei (the mom Lolita type). A woman in early or advancing middle age who wears frilly baby-doll outfits with childish accessories and jewelry. Also known as *obarori* (old maid Lolita).

Manaitakei (the cutting-board type). The flat-chested woman.

Matchokei. The macho type.

Nikushokujoshi (the carnivorous woman). A woman who, were she a man, would be an alpha male.

Nyūbōikei (the new-boy type). A person who either is or looks like a female-to-male transsexual.

Nyūhāfukei (the new-half type). A person who either is or looks like a transvestite or transsexual. Also referred to with the initials *NH-kei,* pronounced *enu-eichi-kei.*

Obankei. The old maid type.

Ō-eru-kei (the OL type). A woman with an "office lady" or secretarial look.

Okamakei (the gay type). The gayish, gay, or gay-looking man.

Onēkei (the sister type). A young woman with very deeply tanned skin, light-brown hair, and showy clothes and accessories. The male version, also with light-brown hair, tan, and expensive, flamboyant clothes is *oniikei* (brother type).

Ora-ora-kei (the I-I type). The rough, "verbal" male—a man or butch lesbian who is aggressive, loud, and verbally abusive in bed. From *ora,* the roughest way of saying "I" in Japanese.

Rezukei (the lesbian type). A lesbian, or a woman or man who looks like one.

Riimankei. A man with a white-collar worker look. *Riman* is short for *sarariman* (salary man).

Rorikei (the Lolita type). Either an underage girl, or a young (and sometimes not so young) woman who dresses or acts underage, wearing baby-doll clothes and accessories, such as white lace umbrellas, or fluffy white fans. There are the wilder *pankurori* (punk Lolitas); *shirorori* (white Lolitas) in white frilly clothes; *kurorori* (black Lolitas) in black frilly clothes; *pinkurori* (pink Lolitas); and the *gosurori,* the Goth Lolitas, with black lips, black nails, and heavy black makeup over white foundation.

Seijunkei (the innocent type). Usually a demure-looking porn actress.

Seinenkei. The young boy type.

Serebukei (the celeb type). The glamorous woman.

Shirikonkei (the silicone type). Usually the porn actress with enlarged breasts.

Sōshokukei (the herbivorous type). The submissive and shy man, who is the opposite of the alpha-male go-getter.

Sujikinkei (the sinewy-muscle type). A man with a defined, muscular body.

Sūpāgatchiri kei (the super bulked-up type). Also shortened to *SG-kei,* pronounced *esujii kei.*

Surimukei. The slim type.

Yarōkei. The ruffian type.

(NEKURA. Depressed or negative.)

While a young American is "down," in a "blue funk," or has assumed a "prune face," a young Japanese with similar symptoms is diagnosed by his fashionable friends as *nekura*. This new, modish word originated from the phrase *ne ga kurai*, "the root is dark," and is closely related to its equally "in" antonym *neaka*, "bright-rooted," reserved for peppy and positive individuals. In these cases, "root" refers to a person's character, personality, or nature.

> *Kanojo'tte itsumo nekura na no? Soretomo ima dake?*
> Has she always been so negative, or is it new?
> *Sonna ni nekura ni natte 'nai de! Odorō ze! Tanjōbi jan!*
> Don't be so depressing! C'mon, let's dance! It's your birthday!

Nekura gave rise to the school-slang abbreviation *nekku*, also meaning "blue" or "in the dumps."

> *Hott'okeba! Ano ko kyō nekku!*
> Lay off it, man! The poor kid's in the dumps!
> *Atashi anta sonna ni nekku ni naru toki daikirai!*
> I hate it when you get so bummed!

Another notable term is *kuradishonaru*, which together with its peers *nekura* and *nekku* also belongs to the *kurai* ("dark" or "gloomy") group of words. Like many of the most "in" Japanese slang words today, it is an Anglo-Japanese alloy, a fusion of *kurai* and *toradishonaru*, "traditional."

The poor individual for whom *kuradishonaru* is reserved is regarded as gloomy and depressed precisely because he or she is "traditional," which in modern Japan is tantamount to being "just too uncool for words."

> *Kuradishonaru gyaru nante dēto shitaku nai.*
> I don't wanna go on a date with such a nerdy girl.
> *Kanojo debu da shi, busu da shi, kuradishonaru da shi,*
> *moderu naritai shi! Saiaku!*
> She's fat, she's ugly, she's a nerd, and she wants to be a
> model! P-l-l-l-ease!

A depressed person who is a wet blanket at fun get-togethers could be denounced in fashionable if slangy Japanese with the verb *būtareru*. The etymology of this expression is *bū*, as in *būbū yū*, "to complain" or "to grumble," and *tareru*, "to drop" or "to let go."

> *Sonna ni būtareru na yo!*
> Stop whining!
> *Ano ko ni tomodachi ga inai no mo atarimae da yo na!*
> *Itsumo būtareru kara sa!*
> I'm not surprised that girl has no friends! She's always
> pissing and moaning!

Another unfortunate state to be in is what is known as *busukureru*. The depressed, down-and-out individual who is so devastated about something or other that his face clenches up in a sour grimace—the derivation of *busukureru* is *busu*, "ugly," and *kureru*, "to be overcome with" or "to abandon oneself to."

> *Busukureru no yamero yo! Chanto meiku shite, issho ni*
> *dekakeyō ze!*
> Why don't you just get over it! Put some makeup on and
> let's hit the scene!
> *Uchi no kurasu no onna-domo minna busukurete bak-*
> *kari ite! Zenzen tsumannē!*
> Those girls in our class are such downers! They're a total
> drag!

Another word reserved for the saturnine or the morose is *yande'ru*, originating from *yamu*, "to be taken ill."

> **Yande'ru yatsu!**
> What a grim guy!
> **Kono ongaku honto yande'ru yo!**
> This music's just too down!

A stronger word reserved for a truly dismal state of affairs is *do-tsubo*, "large pot." It is a hardy slang word that is used as readily by a Yakuza boss when things go wrong as by a thirteen-year-old schoolgirl miffed about having failed a test. A typical idiomatic usage would be *do-tsubo ni hamaru*, "to fall into a large pot."

> **Ore moshi kotoshi daigaku ni hairenakattara, jinsei dotsubo da yo na!**
> If I don't get into college this year, my life'll be the pits!
> **Kanojo himo to ōgenka shichatte! Mō do-tsubo!**
> She had a big row with her pimp! She's in for it!

(NUSUMU. To steal.)

Nusumu is the standard word for stealing. It can be used in general for most types of theft. The character for *nusu* is written with the two ideograms "next" and "plate," suggesting that the primary idea when the character was originally composed in China was swiping food from someone else's plate.

> **Anta kore doko kara nusunda no?**
> Where did you steal that from?
> **Atashi no sukāto nusunda deshō? Kaeshina yo!**
> You stole my skirt, right? Give it back!

The other main phrase for stealing is *dorobō suru*. *Dorobō* can mean both "thief" and "theft." It originated as a contraction of the somewhat blasphemous *toru bōzu*, "filching priest." Today *dorobō* is written in two ways: *doro*, "mud," and *bō*, "priest," and more recently and less sacrilegiously, *doro*, "mud," and *bō*, "stick."

> *Aitsu wa dōtokushin no kakera mo nē! Mitamono nandemo dorobō yagaru!*
> That guy's got no morals! He'll steal anything that's in front of him!
> *Atashi tatta no nifun kuruma hanareta dake na no ni, kuruma dorobō sarechatta yo!*
> I just left the car there for two minutes, and it was stolen!

When someone "pilfers," "swipes," or "rips off" smaller objects, the mot juste is *kapparau*. It originally evolved from the two words *kaku*, "to scratch," and *karau*, "to brush together": the image of the character suggesting a feverish scraping together of goods, followed by a dash for the open.

> *Ano yarō ore no tokei mata kapparaiyagatte! Bukkorosu!*
> That asshole swiped my watch again! I'm gonna kill him!
> *Dare ga anta no saifu kapparatta no? Shitte'ru?*
> Who filched your wallet, d'you know?

In the same crowd of common light-theft words is a term of somewhat ruder etymology, *nekobaba*, "cat shit." When an individual is guilty of "cat shitting," the implication is that he has "pocketed" or "copped" small but important things, usually money. The inspiration for "cat shitting" as a synonym for swiping is that cats quickly cover their tracks after defecating and act as if nothing happened.

> *Shinjirarenē! Ittai ikura aitsu nekobaba shiyagatta'n da?*
> I don't believe this! How much did this guy swipe?

> **Ano shin'iri no onna, reji no kane zettai nekobaba shite'run dakara!**
> That new woman keeps filching money from the register!

The main word for shoplifting is *mambiki*. In modern times it is written with the characters *man*, "ten thousand," and *hiku*, "to snatch," but it originated as the rural term *ma ni hiku*, "thinning out vegetables in a field" (literally "taking from in-between").

> **Saikin mambiki yarinikui yo nē! Ironna tokoro ni kamera wa tsuite'ru shi sā!**
> Shoplifting's becoming kinda hard lately! There's all kinda cameras and stuff!
> **Shinu hodo hazukashii yo! Obā-chan mambiki shite'ru toki tsukamatchatte sā!**
> I thought I was gonna die, I was so embarrassed! They caught granny shoplifting!

A slangier synonym for shoplifting, favored by the younger street crowd, is *chomboru*, inspired by the expression *chombo*, "mistake" or "lapse."

> **Ano kuchibeni anta chombotta yatsu?**
> Is that the lipstick you filched?
> **Omē yo! Kanojo chomboru no ga sugē hayē'n da ze! Uaa!**
> Dude! She's ace at swiping stuff! Wow!

The young criminal set often prefers not to call a spade a spade, or in this case call filching filching. This penchant is clearly visible in what are at the moment some of the "in" street euphemisms for stealing: *kau*, "to buy"; *kaimono suru*, "to go shopping"; and the ominous *shigoto ni iku*, "to go to work."

> **Nani, kono meiku zembu katta? Iikagen ni shiro yo!**
> What, you "bought" all that makeup? I wish you wouldn't do that!
> **Aitsu resutoran de kegawa no kōto sanchaku kaimono shita no.**
> He swiped three fur coats from that restaurant.
> **Shigoto ni itte kuru yo.**
> I'm just going on a quick job.

Another street word for shoplifting is *dekigokoro*, "sudden impulse." As the word suggests, it is an unpremeditated act: you see it, you want it, you swipe it.

> **Sūpā ni iku to dōshite mo dekigokoro shitaku natchau!**
> Whenever I go down to the supermarket I get this urge to filch things!
> **Shinjirarenai! Ano obatarian dekigokoro shichau nante!**
> I can't believe that old bitch swipes things!

The most vivid words for theft in Japanese belong to *ingo*, the "hidden language" of the underworld. These words are thieves' "shoptalk" and not generally understood off the streets. An example is *warau*, "to laugh," as in *Kore waratta?* (You laughed that?), "You stole that?"

> **Omē ga waratta kuruma kakuii jan!**
> The car you swiped's real cool!
> **Omae waratta mon' doko ni kakushite'n da yo?**
> Where d'you stash the stuff you boosted?

In the same class of *ingo* words we have *tsumu*, "to pluck," and *giru*, short for *negiru*, "to drive a bargain."

Ore tsunda mono zembu utte, chitto kane kasegō to motte'ru.
I'm gonna sell all the stuff I ripped off and make a bit of money.
Kono kane zembu dok'kara gitta'n do?
Where did you swipe all this cash from?

(OKAMA. Homosexual.)

This is the most widely used derogatory word for homosexual in Japan, parallel to English expressions like "fag" or "queer," though like these words in America, *okama* is gaining in acceptability among gay circles in Japan.

Okama originated from the word *kama,* a word for "rice pot" in use since the Heian period (794–1185). The first step in its development into the modern slang word was when dialects like Harima, Ibaraki, Toyama, and Yamaguchi added the honorific *o-* prefix and decreed it to mean "ass."* From this, by somewhat unkind association, the slang word for "homosexual" crystallized.

> **Soko no okama omē no koto zutto mite'ru ae.**
> That faggot there keeps checking you out.
> **Okama datta'tte? Kekkon shite'ru to omotte'tta!**
> He's queer? I thought he was married!

In order to soften the untoward connotation of the noun *okama,* some people opt for the politer *okama-san,* "Mr. Faggot."

---

*Some dialects, notably the Sanno, the Ōtawara, the Haga-gun, and the Kamitogagun, regarded the *kama* rice pot, with the added *o-* prefix, as more representative of the vagina, while the Shizuoka and the Ashikaga dialects went their own way, using *kama* to mean "dark, hidden secret."

Although *okama-san* may be a modest gesture toward being civil, the modern and the open-minded prefer the more neutral *gei*, "gay."

> **Ano hito okama-san yo.**
> That guy's a fag.
> **Kono bā wa okama-san shika inai yo. Hoka ni ikō.**
> This bar is full of queers. Let's go someplace else.
> **Omae to hanashiteta okamasan-tachi nani mono?**
> Who were those fags talking to you?

When something or someone behaves in a "gay" or "faggoty" manner, *okama* can be changed into an adjective by using suffixes like *-ppoi*, *-rashii*, and *-kusai*, to create *okamappoi*, "faggotish"; *okamarashii*, "faggotlike"; and *okamakusai*, "smelling of faggot."

> **Aitsu-ra okamappoi nā.**
> Those guys are real faggoty.
> **Sonna okamappoku odoranaide yo—minna mite'ru yo!**
> Don't dance like such a queen—everyone's looking!
> **Ano ossan okamarashii koe de hanasu yo na.**
> That old guy talks in a real swishy voice.
> **Kono sūtsu sugē okamakusai jan.**
> This suit's like really queer.
> **Chotto sono kutsu okamakusai jan—kaete yo.**
> Those shoes are kinda faggoty—take them back.
> **Nande minna ore no koto okamakusai'tte iu'n darō?**
> Why does everyone think I'm a faggot?

A more modern *okama* adjective is the witty high-school invention *okamachikku*, literally "faggot-ic," the *-chikku* ending having been borrowed from words such as *romanchikku* (romantic) or *akurobachikku* (acrobatic). It can also mean "gayish."

> **Nē! Omē sonna okamachikku na no yamete kurenai?**
> Will you cut that faggoty shit?
> **Kotoshi no ryūkō no fuku wa minna okamachikku da.**
> This year's fashion's so gayish.

A very popular deprecatory word implying that the homosexual in question is passive and effeminate is *onē*, "sister," often used in gay circles in its vocative form *Onē-san!* as a cute and girlish form of address. *Onē kotoba* (sister words) is the term for gay slang, with its own specialized vocabularies, risqué banter, and exaggerated feminine grammar (preferring the feminine "I" pronoun *atashi*, for instance) with straitlaced, traditional feminine word endings.

> **Nani ano debu no onē! Ittai nani mono!**
> Get a load of that fat queen! Who does girlfriend think she is?
> **Onē-san! Mite, mite! Oishisō!**
> Ooh, girl! Lookie! He's tasty!

A homosexual slang word that is practical for establishing who is passive and who is not, especially in chance encounters, is *uke*, from *ukemi*, "receiving body" or "passive."

> **Anta uke?**
> You a bottom?
> **Mayonaka sugi ni, uke-ra wa minna ano bā e kuridasun da.**
> After midnight, all the bottom boys get together at that bar.

Another popular Japanese word for "queen" is *neko*. Though most people assume that *neko* comes from the Japanese word for cat, and that this term for homosexual is inspired perhaps by a cat's feline and feminine grace, *neko* is said to come from *neko-guruma* (wheelbarrow), and the initial idea of using the term to mean a passive homosexual was inspired by the concept that a wheelbarrow's handles could be seen as legs, with the man pushing the wheelbarrow standing between them.

> ***Ano neko itsumo kao no ii otoko mono ni suru! Dō yaru'n darō?***
> That fruit always gets good-looking guys! How does she do it?
> ***Ano neko yakamashii!***
> That queen's so loud!

The related expression *oraneko* (I-queen) is used for very masculine men, who use the toughest first personal Japanese pronoun, *ora* (I), but who are in fact passive in bed. An unkinder synonym is *bakeneko* (monster queen). The exact opposite of the *oraneko* and *bakeneko* is the *barineko,* "all-out queen."

> ***Aitsu sugē otokoppoi kedo, jitsu wa oraneko da yo.***
> He looks like a real man, but he's just a muscle queen.
> ***Oi, miro yo! Ano barineko onna no fuku kite'ru zē!***
> Hey, check it out! That queen's actually wearing a dress!

The opposite of *neko* is *tachi,* short for *tachiyaku,* a long-standing expression from the Japanese Kabuki theater signifying the dynamic male role—the fighter with his sword ready for action. (As *tachi* is also the word for a traditional Japanese sword, it is also used to refer to a large or erect penis.) *Baritachi* is the all-out "top," while *boi tachi* is a twink top, or very young top, *femu tachi* is a "fem top," an active homosexual whose femininity gives the misleading impression of passivity.

While a *neko* is effeminate and a "bottom," the *tachi* is the masculine "top."

An interesting variation is *netachi,* a melding of *neko* and *tachiyaku.* The *netachi* is the homosexual who acts feminine, but (to the surprise of the chance partner) prefers the active role in bed.

> **Nē, mite! Ano tachi hoshii wa! Kawaii!**
> Ooh, look! I want that hunk! He's cute!
> **Anna otoko yamena! Netachi yo!**
> Forget that guy! He acts like a lady, but he's a top!

Ribāshiburu (reversible), or more commonly, *riba* for short, are men who are "versatile," ready to adopt either position—known as *seku* (from "sex") in gay and lesbian slang. The versatile gay is also known as *ribako* (reversible child), particularly when he is young and attractive. *Ribatachi* is the man who is a "versatile top," and *ribaneko* is the "versatile bottom."

A newer *okama* word on the scene is *ribugama*, an amalgam of *ribu* (gay lib) and *okama*, and is used about gay men who are very active on the gay lib scene. But the strangest of the new words is perhaps *nekama*, short for *netto okama*, "Internet queer," and refers to men (not necessarily homosexual) who pose as women in chat rooms, Internet forums, and online games.

(OMANKO. Vagina.)

Omanko is to Japanese what "cunt" is to English. Both words are of ancient lineage, and began as legitimate words. "Cunt" enjoys an illustrious pedigree, with forerunners such as the Latin *cunnus*. *Omanko*, it is argued, has an even more distinguished background, although its exact etymology is still being wrangled over. The initial *O*, all sides agree, is the euphemistic honorific that is sometimes dispensed with for an earthier effect (as in *Manko yarō ze!* "Let's get us some cunt!").

After this initial point of agreement, the fight among linguists begins. "Where does *omanko's man* come from?" is the burning question. One of the most outlandish theories was advanced by the eccentric South American Japanologist F. Perez

de Vega. Staunchly believing that the Inca Empire was found-
ed by ancient Japanese warriors, he argues that the *man* of
omanko comes from the Guarani Indians in Ecuador, *man* being their word for spirit. Popular linguist Kawasaki Shinji argues that *man* is even older, being a Sumerian word for womb.
Notwithstanding its disputed pedigree, today *omanko* is the
most popular term in Japan for the female organ.

> ***Chotto sukāto makutte miro yo. Omanko sawatte yaru
> kara sa.***
> Lift your skirt a little. I wanna feel your pussy.
> ***Kono dii-bui-dii de onna no omanko honto ni marumie
> da ze!***
> In this DVD you can see this woman's cunt head-on!
> ***Kanojo no omanko wa itsumo jūshii da!***
> Her cunt's always juicy!

The *man* of *omanko* appears in many word combinations:

> **Kechaman**, from **kechappumanko**, "ketchup vagina." A
> menstruating vagina. Also known as *akaman*, "red vagina."
> **Ketsuman** (anus vagina). An anus that is used for sex (as
> if it were a vagina).
> **Kuchiman** (mouth vagina). A mouth that is used for sex.
> **Manchira** (vagina flash). Catching an unexpected glance at
> a vagina.
> **Mange** (vagina hair). Also known as *andahea*, "underhair."
> **Mankojiru** (vagina soup). Smegma.
> **Mankosuji** (cunt line). The clearly visible line of a vagina
> when a woman wears tight shorts of thin fabric or lycra,
> known in American slang as "cameltoe."
> **Manshamēru** (vagina photo e-mail). An e-mail with an
> attachment of a photograph of a vagina.
> **Mantaku** (vagina print). The vagina is painted and a print
> is made. A sex-trade service that has also developed into
> an art form.

Nodo-man (neck vagina). Deep-throating.

Sokuman (instant vagina). In Internet hookups, when people have sexual intercourse immediately upon meeting. This is also known as *sokuapo-sokuman*, "instant appointment, instant vagina."

Tachiman (standing vagina). Sex in a standing position.

Teman (hand vagina). Male masturbation, using the hand as if it were a vagina.

Tetsuman (iron vagina). A sex-trade hostess with an unusual amount of endurance.

Yariman (sex vagina). A promiscuous woman.

Yubiman (finger vagina). Male masturbation, using the fingers as if they were a vagina. Also, in the sex trade, when the man inserts a finger into the vagina of the *kompanyon* (companion), or hostess.

What *omanko* is to standard Japanese, *omeko* is to the Osaka dialect. In the unlikely event that it is written in characters, the characters *me*, "woman," and *ko*, "child," are used. The etymology of this word is also in dispute. One of the more interesting ideas is that *omeko* comes from the statue of the god Omeko Daikoku in Osaka, whose right hand shows the thumb protruding from a clenched fist. *Omeko* is now widely used outside Osaka when a rougher, cruder alternative to *omanko* is called for.

Nande atashi no omeko kayukute shōganai no ka na?
I wonder why my snatch is so itchy?
Atashi aitsu ga ii ko ni shitenakya, omeko agenai kara.
If he's not a good boy, I won't give him any snatch.

Two other dialect words for the female organ used throughout Japan, particularly in the sex trade, are *soso* and *ososo*. These words were originally used exclusively by women as a euphemism. They developed from *sore sore*, "that that," into what was at the time an even meeker *so so*. Today few users of *soso* are aware of its demure background, and they savor its attractive alliterative quality. But beware! Regardless of their euphemistic past, *soso* and *ososo* have the same jarring impact on the well-bred Japanese ear as *omeko* or *omanko*.

> **Atashi aitsu ni saseru no wa soso sawaraseru made yo.**
> The only thing I let him do is touch my twat.
> **Sekken de ososo arau no kirai. Datte kasa kasa ni natchau yo.**
> I hate washing my pussy with soap. It gets all like dried out.

Two more slang words for vagina are *bobo* and its related *obobo*, which come from the island of Kyushu. Like *soso* and *ososo*, *bobo* and *obobo* owe much of their success in the sex trade to their upbeat, alliterative ring.

An elaboration on *bobo* is *sarabobo*, which can have two meanings: "new *bobo*," meaning the organ of a virgin or very young woman, or "plate *bobo*," in which case the organ in question is "platelike" (that is, wide but not deep).

> **Aitsu neta ato demo, zettai ni bobo misete kurenai.**
> Even after we slept together, she still doesn't let me see her pussy.
> **Shojo no sarabobo'tte shimari ga ii kara ii yo na!**
> The great thing about a virgin's twat is that it's nice and tight!

Another noteworthy onomatopoeic word for vagina is *bebe*, a word that originated in the Oyama, Kanuma, Ōtawara, and Yaita dialects.* *Bebe* belongs to the same group of sex-trade terms that, due to their pleasant ring, have risen from the

---

*Its close relatives *hehe* and *pepe* did not make it on the national scene, partly because in some villages, confusingly enough, these words also mean "penis" or "sexual intercourse."

comparative obscurity of the provinces to national notoriety. *Bebe* also has the advantage over *bobo* and *soso* of sounding foreign, if not French.

> *Aitsu atashi no bebe ni dake kyōmi aru'n da yo ne! Futsū no otoko dakara ne!*
> All he's interested in is my snatch! Typical of men!
> *Ore sutorippā no me no mae ni suwatta kara yo! Bebe marumie datta!*
> Man! I sat right in front of that stripper! I could see her twat inside out!

Three other vulgar words for vagina are *kanko* and *okanko*, originally from the Sanno dialect, and *ochanko*, from Tokushima. They are favored in other regions too because they rhyme with the standard words for vagina, *manko* and *omanko*.

> *Hajime no uchi kanojo no kanko ga kawaite'ta kara chotto itakatta.*
> At first it hurt a bit 'cause her cunt was dry.
> *Atashi okanko ni tampon ireru toki no kanji daikirai!*
> I hate the feeling of a tampon up my cunt!
> *Aitsu panstu haite nē kara, minna ni ochanko mietchimau.*
> She wasn't wearing panties, so everyone could see her cunt.

Among the provincial words that have made it onto city backstreets, there are also expressions that are not as widely known as their onomatopoetic relatives. *Sane* is one of these words for vagina; it arrived on the national slang scene after enjoying widespread popularity in the Yaita and Utsunomiya dialects. Another word for the female organ is *shimo*, which was actually inspired by one of the alternative pronunciations of the character for "down" (usually read *shita*).

> *Chotto sane hippan'no yamete yo! Itai jan!*
> Will you stop tugging at my snatch! It hurts!
> *Kono mizugi katta kedo kirenai yo! Shimo marumie!*
> I can't wear this swimsuit I bought! You can see my crack!

(ONABE. Lesbian.)

One of the derogative Japanese words for lesbian that over the past decade has become an increasingly accepted term is *onabe,* "pan," a pun on the Japanese word for homosexual, *okama,* "pot." Though *onabe* is still often considered a slur when used by non-lesbians, it is being adopted in Japanese lesbian circles, much as "dyke" has been by English-speaking lesbians. Unlike the English word "dyke," however, *onabe* still tends to be used more for very masculine women, and also for *efu-tii-emu (FtM),* "female-to-male transsexuals," also known as *toransu* (trans); *nyūboi* (new boy); and *nyūgai* (new guy).*

> *Onabe ka, bōisshu gāru wakarinikui.*
> I'm not sure if she's a dyke, or just a straight butch girl.
> *Zettai sonna furifuri fuku kinnai yo, ore hyaku pāsento onabe dakara.*
> I'd never wear frilly shit like that, I'm 100 percent dyke.
> *Otoko ka to omottara, nyūboi datta.*
> I thought it was a guy, but she turned out to be a trans.
> *Shōkurabu Aporo de nyūboi no boshū shite'ru mitai yo.*
> I hear that the Apollo Cabaret's looking for FtM performers.

An insider word for transgender or transsexual is *tora,* "tiger," a pun on the first half of the word *toransu* (transgender).

> *Koko tora bakkari de, onna no ki inai ne.*
> The place is full of FtMs, no women at all.

---

*Male-to-female transsexuals are called *nyūhāfu,* "new-half."

Horu, short for "hormones," and *ope,* short for "operation," are used among Japanese FtM to specify individuals who are undergoing hormone treatment or have undergone chest reconstruction surgery. Depending on the context, *ope* is also used to indicate phalloplasty—*inkei keiseijutsu* (penis construction)—or metoidioplasty—*inkakuinkei keiseijyutu* (clitoris to penis construction).

> **Saisho ni horu yatte, shibaraku shite ope.**
> First you do hormones, then after a while comes the operation.
> **Aitsu horu-ope shite kara, otokoppoku natta yo na.**
> Since his hormones and operation, he's got a real manly look.

Just as "dyke bar," "dyke march," or "dykes on bikes" are accepted lesbian terminology in English, Japanese word compounds with *onabe,* or *nabe,* are now becoming more frequent: *Onabe kurabu* (dyke club); *onabe saito* (dyke website); *onabe bā* (dyke bar); and *onabe shō pabu,* literally "dyke-show pub," a popular form of drag cabaret in which women who can pass as men put on a floor show for a predominantly straight audience.

Onabe gudzu (dyke goods) are quality accessories used by masculine lesbians and female-to-male transsexuals wishing to dress as men. Some popular *onabe gudzu* are:

> **Baribari** is a breast binder that can flatten a woman's chest. It is also known as *torabando,* "trans band."
> **Nabesapo** (dyke support) is a compression vest that flattens the breasts.
> **Nabeshātsu** (dyke shirt), and *torashātsu* or *toransushātsu* (transsexual shirts), are masculine shirts specifically tailored to deemphasize breasts.
> **Nūchin** (nude penis) is a flaccid silicone penis worn with a belt or affixed to the pubic region for a realistic male

> crotch look. They also come in the form of *nūchintsuki*
> *pantsu,* which are underpants, briefs, or boxer shorts with
> built-in flaccid penises.
> **Tachishōben herupā** (standing urination helper), often
> shortened to *tachishon herupā,* is a funnel device with a
> spout (which in luxury models looks like a flaccid penis)
> with which a female-to-male transsexual can urinate at a
> urinal.

A special slang word used in lesbian circles to specify the
more masculine dyke (who is "active" in bed) is *tachi.* Like the
male gay word *tachi,* which is used for tops or "active" homo-
sexuals, *tachi* comes from the Kabuki theater, where *tachiyaku*
designates the dynamic masculine role.

> **Kanojo no gārufurendo'tte sugoku tachi da mon ne.**
> Her girlfriend's a real bull dyke.
> **Ryō wa otachi dakara, zettai doresu o kinai darō ne!**
> Ryō's a bull dyke, she'd never wear a dress!

The opposite of the masculine-acting *tachi* is the more
femu "femme" lesbian. As in gay male slang, *neko* (wheelbarrow) is used for lesbians who prefer the passive role.

> **Ano neko doko de hirotte kita no?**
> Where d'you pick that femme up?
> **Miho wa tsuyoi onna no koto suki ja nai no. Femu ga suki**
> **nan da yo.**
> Suzuko's not into butch women, she likes femmes.

Tachi (butch) and *neko* (fem) are also used as the sexual
role an individual prefers. *Seku* (from *sekushuaritei,* "sexuality")
is the slang word for "sexual role."

Butch lesbians will often use masculine personal pronouns
such as *boku* ("I," used by younger males); *ore* ("I," used by tougher,

more mature males); and even *ora* ("I," used by very rough men and gangsters), while fem lesbians will use the standard *watashi* for "I," or the feminine *atashi*.

> **Ore no seku wa tachi.**
> I'm a top.
> **Anta no seku wa nan nano?**
> What role are you?
> **Atashi no seku riba yo.**
> I'm versatile.

Tachi (butch) and *neko* (fem) come in various gradations. *Baritachi* (all-out butch lesbian) is a woman who under no circumstances would opt for a passive or feminine stance in her behavior or sexuality. Because she dresses in men's clothes, the *baritachi* is also referred to as *misu dandei* (Miss Dandy), as are sometimes women who have undergone the sex-change operation. Also butch is the *dana* (from *danna*, "husband" or "master"), who is usually attracted to fem or "lipstick lesbians." The *danazu,* on the other hand, are very butch women who are attracted to other very butch women.

Another lesbian-slang synonym for butch women who like other butch women is *nabehomo* (dyke homo) or *homotachi* (homo butch), the idea being that, just like homosexual men are interested in other men, the masculine *homotachi* lesbian is interested in other masculine women.

Jaritachi (brat butch) is a young, boyish lesbian, usually rough and rowdy, and is used in lesbian circles in a pejorative way, while the *boishutachi* (boyish butch) is the attractive girl who looks and acts like a boy.

Less firm in her masculinity is the *ribatachi,* "versatile butch," who is usually active in bed, but occasionally passive, and the *sukatachi* (a contraction of *sukātotachi,* "skirt butch"), a butch and active lesbian who will occasionally wear a skirt.

At the other end of the scale are the *femi* (femmy); *femu* (fem); or *femufemu*, the feminine "lipstick lesbians" who wear skirts and makeup. The doubling of *femu* in *femufemu* is considered cute and appealing, and consequently is often used by girlish lesbians to describe themselves.

Straight men who habitually hang out with lesbians— known as lezbros in American slang—are called in lesbian circles *osusu* (soot). The etymology of *osusu*: the word for dyke, *onabe*, actually means "pan," and *osusu*, "soot," is something that doggedly sticks to pans.

The newest *onabe* on the scene is the *nenabe*, from *netto nabe*, "Internet dyke," a woman who poses as a man in chat rooms, online games, and other virtual forums.

(ORUGASUMU. Orgasm.)

In the 1870s, German doctors arriving in Japan as part of the Meiji-era Westernization brought with them German medical terms like *shokku*, for "shock," *asupirin*, for "aspirin," and *orugasumusu*, from the German *Orgasmus*, which, by the way, is still the official Japanese dictionary word. (Aside from euphemisms such as *saikōchō*, "climax" or "peak," and *kyokudo no kōfun*, "extreme excitement," Japanese has no official native words for orgasm.)

Since its introduction into Japanese, *orugasumusu* has been treated with all the deference appropriate to a long-winded foreign medical term that was thought to sound too authoritative for colloquial speech. This changed when the media and fashionable magazines developed an interest in orgasm and started using *orugasumu*, a shortened version of the German original, or *ōgasumu*, the Japanese pronunciation of the English word. As some magazines might write:

> **Hajimete no sekkusu de orugasumu o erareru koto wa mazu arimasen.**
> During one's first sexual experience it is very rare to experience orgasm.
> **Naze watashi wa ōgasumu o kanjinai no deshō?**
> Why can I not experience orgasm?

With the gentle prompting of the popular question-and-answer sections of teen magazines and other popular periodicals that offer sexual advice and enlightenment, the two semiofficial words for "orgasm," *ōgasumu* and *orugasumu,* now appear in slangier speech.

> **Kanojo wa ōgasumu ni tasshita toki, sugē uairudo ni natta.**
> When she had her orgasm, she went totally wild.
> **Kinō yokatta ze! Kanojo to ore dōji ni orugasumu kanjita mon!**
> Yesterday was great! We had an orgasm at the same time!

In relaxed conversation, Japanese slang speakers often prefer stronger native words. One of the more unconventional but pithy terms for orgasm used on the streets is *rariru,* "to flip out," a term usually connected with a drug high.

> **Atashi itsumo raritta furi shite'ru kara, kare manzoku nan da!**
> I always pretend to get off just to make him feel good!
> **Ore-tachi pettingu shite'ta dake na no ni, ore raritchatta!**
> Although we were just making out I really shot my wad!

A strong slang word from the red-light district, used exclusively in reference to male orgasm, is *naku,* "to cry" or "to howl." This expression is usually used by the "soap girls" of the

Soapland establishments and by sex-club hostesses in discussing their clientele's orgasms.

> **Kyaku no asoko yasashiku ijitte yaru to, motto hayaku nakaserareru yo.**
> If you rub your client's dick gently, chances are he'll shoot his wad quicker.
> **Anta nō naichatta no! Hayasugi ja nai?**
> What, you got off already? That was a bit quick, wasn't it?

A special term reserved for those times when a couple reaches orgasm simultaneously is *hamoru,* an idiom borrowed from the show-business world, where it is used to refer to successful musical harmonizing between a male and a female singer.

> **Atashi hamonnai toki wa kirai.**
> I hate it when we don't come together.
> **Sekkusu de ichiban no pointo wa hamoreru ka dō ka da yo! Deshō?**
> The most important thing about sex is coming together! Right?

When a man ejaculates more than once, there is a term popular with the red-light crowd specifying the exact number of orgasms experienced. *Nukani* refers to two orgasms; *nukasan,* to three; *nukayon,* to four; *nukago,* to five; and a superhuman *nukaroku,* to six. All these terms are a contraction of *nukanai,* "not taking out," with any number as a suffix (*-san,* "3"; *-yon,* "4"; *-go,* "5"; and so on). The literal translation of a statement like *nukaroku* would read: "Without pulling out, I came six times in a row."

> **Ore sugē kōfun shite'ta kara nukasan shichatta yo!**
> I was so turned-on that I came three times in a row!
> **Ima made no saikō kiroku wa ano onna to nukayon da yo.**
> My best record so far was with that woman when I came four times in a row.

(PIN. Erection.)

The most common slang terms for erection are:

> **Tatsu.** To stand.
> **Ōkiku naru.** To become big.
> **Genki ni naru.** To become lively.
> **Dekaku naru.** To become large.
> **Kataku naru.** To become hard.

Any of these expressions can be used in the following examples:

> **Ore no chimpo tatta!**
> My dick got hard!
> **Aitsu no asoko ōkiku natta!**
> His thing got hard!
> **Aitsu ikinari genki ni natta!**
> He suddenly got hard!

Pin is a sound word much like the English "boing," and is often used in conjunction with these terms to suggest the liveliness of the event and the immediacy of horniness.

> **Pin to ōkiku natta!**
> He suddenly got a rod on!

> **Pin to kataku natta!**
> He got rock hard!

The next step in *pin*'s slang evolution came when it broke loose from the other words for erection and became an idiom in its own right, useful for specifying a healthy, vibrant stiffness.

> **Ore no asoko sa, basu ni notte'ru to itsumo pin to natchimau!**
> You know, my dick always gets hard when I ride on buses!
> **Atashi kare ni yokkakatta no! Sō shitara aitsu ikinari pin to natte'n no!**
> I rubbed against him and he immediately got a rod on!

In school yards and on college campuses, *pin* developed even further, becoming *pinpin-chan*, "Mr. Boing Boing," a cute term for an erect penis, or for a young man's penis that is ready to rise at the drop of a hat.

> **Kare no pinpin-chan sugē kawaii'n dakara.**
> I think his willy's cute when it gets hard.
> **Kare asa okiru to itsumo pinpin-chan ni natte'ru.**
> His pecker's always stiff in the morning.

Another term for vibrant erections, popular with the *bōsōzoku* (motorcycle gangs) and other young Japanese motorcycle enthusiasts, is *uiri*, "wheelie," a word of American motorcyclist origin referring to the biker's precarious but flashy stunt of riding on the rear wheel only, with the front wheel raised off the ground.

> **Ano ko ga fuku o nuida totan, ore uiri shichatta!**
> The moment she took her off clothes I got a rod on!

Another word for the erect male member enjoyed by the younger crowd is *kokachin*, believed to derive from *kōka*, "stiffening," and *chin*, "penis."

> **Omē kokachin'tte dore gurai ōkii no? Hakatta koto aru?**
> How big is your dick when it gets hard? Have you measured it?

A modern red-light district favorite for the erect male organ is *hakebune*, "sailing boat."

> **Atashi katai hakebune no otoko ga suki!**
> I like a man with a hard dick!

Cruder red-light words, used to intimate that the penis in question is startlingly large, are *gandaka* and *karidaka*. Both *gan* and *kari* are synonyms for wild goose, *daka*, meaning "high" or "tall."

These words are seasoned *ingo* (criminal slang) expressions, used by people ranging from older, hardened criminals to the younger street crowd, who dotingly imitate the criminal's rough speech patterns.

> **Kinō sōpurando ni ittara, onna ga ore no gandaka massaji suru no umakute, ore sugu itchatta yo.**
> That chick at the Soapland massage place gave my stiff dick such a good work-over that I came immediately.
> **Ore-tachi issho no shawā abite'tara, Ken no yatsu karidaka ni natte'n no! Bukimi!**
> Us guys were taking a shower, and Ken's dork got piss hard! It was weird!

If an erection occurs in the confines of one's trousers, manifesting itself in the form of a prominent bulge, the current slang term of choice would be *tento o haru*, "pitching a tent."*

---

*As a result of this tent motif, it has become common, by extension, to refer to the penis as *tento mushi*, "tent bug," a pun on the word for "ladybird beetle."

Ano sutorippā ga dete kitara, ore sugu tento hatchimatta!
When that stripper came out, my pants bulged instantly!
Kawaisō na yatsu! Atashi no me no mae de tento hatte'ru no!
The poor bastard! Right in front of me his dick bulged in his pants!

(REZU. Lesbian.)

The formal term used in referring to lesbians is *rezubian*, which is preferred in lesbian circles to the more official native terms *joseidōseiaisha* (female homosexual person) or *dōseiai no onna* (homosexual woman).

> *Uchi no oya atashi ga rezubian da'tte shitta toki, sugoi shokku uketa kedo.*
> When my folks found out I was a lesbian, they got a real shock.
> *Ano hoteru de rezubian pātei aru kara, ikanai?*
> There's a lesbian party at that hotel, shall we go?

While *rezubian* is the formal term, the most common expression is the contraction *rezu*, analogous to English words like "dyke" or "lez." *Rezu* is used both in lesbian and straight circles.

> *Atashi rezu yo! Dakara nan da 'tte yū no?*
> So I'm a lez! You have a problem with that?
> *Onna dōshi de sonna ni betta betta suru to, rezu to omowareru yo.*
> If you two girls are all over each other like that, people are gonna think you're lesbians.

Just as the once-offensive word "dyke" was adopted and embraced by lesbian groups in the English-speaking world, *rezu* has increasingly become a term of solidarity in Japan's lesbian community in the first decade of the twenty-first century. It is used in many word combinations.

Bōisshurezu (boyish lesbian). A young, butch lesbian.

Rezubeteran (lesbian veteran). An older woman with experience and know-how.

Rezuchatto. Online lesbian chat.

Rezuderiheru (lesbian delivery "health club"). A lesbian escort or sex-massage service.

Rezu-erohon. Lesbian pornographic book.

Rezufuōrumu. Online lesbian forum.

Rezugē (a contraction of *rezu* and *gēmu*). Lesbian computer game.

Rezuheru (lesbian "health club"). A sex club for women only.

Rezuhoteru. Lesbian hotel.

Rezukaba (lesbian cabaret). A bar for women who are served and entertained by hostesses.

Rezukafue. Lesbian cafe.

Rezukai. Lesbian get-together; lesbian association.

Rezukappuru. Lesbian couple.

Rezukomikku. Lesbian comics.

Rezukurabu. Lesbian club.

Rezumagajin. Lesbian magazine.

Rezumanga. Lesbian manga cartoons. Also *yuri manga* (lily manga)—*yuri* is a traditional Japanese word for lesbian.

Rezumondai. Lesbian issues.

Rezunetto aidoru (lesbian net-idol). Lesbian Internet celebrity or starlet.

Rezupātei. Lesbian party.

Rezusākuru. Lesbian circle.

There are also many *rezu* word-combinations used by the porn industry that are geared toward men who are interested in watching actresses act out lesbian sexual situations. These terms, however, are offensive to many lesbians, who refer to everything pseudo-lesbian as *rezumono*, "lesbian style."

> ***Purorezu*** (lesbian pro wrestlers). A pun on *puroresu*, "pro wrestler."
> ***Rezubatoru*** (lesbian battle). Unlike lesbian wrestling, this usually means aggressive lesbian sex and is a great favorite in pornography.
> ***Rezuchijo*** (lesbian molester). A pornographic genre, in which an aggressive woman molests and sometimes humiliates a more passive one.
> ***Rezu dei bui dei.*** Lesbian DVD.
> ***Rezu erodōga.*** Lesbian porn movie.
> ***Rezu eromassāji.*** Lesbian erotic massage.
> ***Rezu eroshiin.*** Lesbian sex scene.
> ***Rezu fera*** (lesbian fellatio). A "lesbian" sex scene involving the participation of a man.
> ***Rezu san pi*** (lesbian threesome). *San pi* (three-P) is short for "three people." *Rezu yon pi* (four P) would be a foursome.
> ***Rezu saron*** (lesbian salon). Lesbian sex club.
> ***Rezu ohame.*** Lesbian photo sent as an e-mail attachment.

A slightly derogatory word used both by lesbians and nonlesbians is *zūrē* or *zure*, both inversions of *rezu*. More positive and increasingly fashionable in the new millennium is the shortened version of the word "lesbian," *bian* (the "bian" ending of "lesbian").

> ***Ano hitotachi kitto bian yo.***
> The two of them are definitely dykes.
> ***Nē, kanojo wa bian na no, soretomo tada ā yū kakko shiten'no?***
> Is she a dyke, or does she just dress like one?

Though *rezu* was once a pejorative term (and sometimes still is), *bian* has the advantage of being a newer trend-word without derogatory nuance, and so has increasingly come into its own in the first decade of the twenty-first century. It is now being increasingly used in word combinations such as *biankurabu* (lesbian club) and *bianbā* (lesbian bar).

Shufubian (housewife les-*bian*) and *shufurezu* (housewife lesbian) are married housewives who are either bisexual or closeted lesbians.

Parallel to the English slang trend that has turned the noun "dyke" into the verb "to dyke around," the Japanese have extended *rezu* into *rezuru,* which can either mean "to engage in lesbian sex" or "to act like a lesbian."

> *Rezutta koto aru?*
> Have you ever dyked around?
> *Ano ko dare to rezutte'n no?*
> Who's she dyking around with?
> *Nē, itsumo no bā ni itte, chotto rezutte miyō yo!*
> C'mon, let's hit our usual bar and dyke around a bit!
> *Mō sonna ni rezutte'naide yo! Hazukashii ja nai!*
> I wish you wouldn't act like such a dyke! It's so embarrassing!

Rezu can also be made into an adjective, *rezuppoi* ("lesbianlike" or "dykish"), and can be used in expressions such as:

> *Rezuppoi aidoru.* A lesbianlike idol.
> *Rezuppoi funiki.* A dykish ambience.
> *Rezuppoi hito.* A dykish person.
> *Rezuppoi kōdō.* Dykish behavior.
> *Rezuppoi kūkii.* A dykish atmosphere.

Other adjectival forms that are felt to be slightly more offensive are *rezukusai,* or the rougher *rezukusa* (literally, "smelling of lesbian").

Sonna rezuppoi no yamete yo! Minna miru ja nai!
I wish you'd cut out acting like such a dyke! Everyone's
looking!
Aa, 'ya da kono kamigata! Rezukusai yo!
Ooh, I hate this hairstyle! It's so dykish!

(SEISHI. Sperm.)

There are a number of formal words in Japanese for sperm: *seishi*, made up of the characters *sei*, "vitality," and *shi*, "child"; *seieki* (vitality liquid), which in its broader sense means "seminal fluid"; and *superuma*, the English word "sperm."

> **Ki o tsukete yo, hon no chotto no seishi demo ninshin suru'n dakara ne.**
> Careful, even the smallest drop of sperm can make me pregnant.
> **Koko ni tisshu aru kara, chanto seieki fukina yo!**
> Here's some tissue to wipe the sperm off!
> **Kanojo boku no asoko o shaburu no wa daisuki de, kinō mo seishi o nonda.**
> She loves sucking my dick—yesterday she even drank my cum.

Though the imported word *superuma* (sperm) has traditionally been thought of as a technical word, in the last decade it has been enthusiastically adopted in pornographic material, making the word more familiar and exciting among adult-DVD watchers. *Superuma* has even crept into catchy (though perhaps puzzling) porn titles, such as *Kauntdaun Superuma* (Countdown Sperm); *Bōsō Superuma* (Sperm Delusions); *Superumabuanpaia*

(Sperm Vampire); or the clever *Superumania* ("Spermaniac,"or sperm enthusiast).

Another surprising word that also began as a technical term but is now widely used both colloquially and pornographically is *zamen*, from the German word *Samen*, semen.

> **Ano otoko jibun no superuma totte, atashi no karada-jū nurimakutta!**
> That guy took his sperm and rubbed it all over me!
> **Atashi otoko no zamen'tte anna ni shoppai to omowanakatta wa!**
> I didn't realize a guy's sperm was so salty!

On the street, discussion of sperm takes on a livelier turn, and a mass of inventive expressions have found their way into frank conversations. One of these terms is *kodanejiru*, literally "child-seed soup."

> **Ne! Omoun dakedo sa! Kodanejiru'tte otoko ni yotte zen zen aji ga chigaun da yo ne!**
> Have you noticed how, like, each guy's cum tastes different?
> **Kare sugoi kōfun shite'tte, musuko no saki kara kodanejiru chorotto atama dashiten no.**
> He was so excited that a blob of cum oozed out of his dick.

Other soup-related terms predominantly used in sex-trade circles and pornography are *tsuyu*, "broth"; *otokojiru*, "man soup"; *chimpojiru*, "penis soup"; *kintamajiru*, "testicle soup"; *tamajiru*, "balls soup"; and in gay circles, *osujiru*, "male soup."

> **Anta sugoi tsuyu tamatteta ne!**
> You had a lotta cum stored up!
> **Shiitsu ni otokojiru no shimi ga tsuite, torenakunachatta!**
> I can't get those cum stains off the sheets!

> **Ore sono shunkan mō tomerarenakutte, chimpojiru tobashichatta!**
> I couldn't hold back anymore, my man-juice just spurted out!
> **Chotto mattete! Kuchibiru ni osujiru tsuichatta no fuku kara!**
> Wait a sec! I'm just gonna wipe the man-juice off my lips!

A group of modern milk-related words for sperm are *miruku,* the English "milk"; the rougher *namamiruku,* "raw milk"; *otokomiruku,* "man milk"; *chimpo miruku* and *maramiruku,* both meaning "dick milk"; and *karupisu,* "Calpis," a popular milky soft drink.

Preejaculatory fluid is technically known as *nyōdōkyuseneki* (bulbourethral-gland fluid), a cumbersome term that few people know or use, preferring *gamanjiru,* "patience soup," or *dai-ichi chimpojiru,* "first penis soup."

(SEN. Chasers.)

In American slang, a "chaser" is someone who has a particularly strong preference for a certain type: the "chubby chaser" prefers a heftier build in a partner, the "tranny chaser" is interested in transsexuals or transvestites, and the "cub chaser" likes hairy, young, husky youths. Though there are many different types of American chasers, they cannot compete with the spectacular array of Japanese chasers. The Japanese *-sen*—as in *senmonka,* "specialist"—can be of either sex (but is more often than not male):

Ajisen (Asia chasers). Those who prefer partners from East Asian countries other than Japan. Also *ajiasen.*
Bususen (ugly chasers). Also *B-sen,* pronounced *biisen.*
Daresen (somebody chasers). Those interested in any and every type.

Debusen (chubby chasers). Also *D-sen,* pronounced *diisen.* In gay slang, *egusen.*

Fukesen (age chasers). Prefers older men or women.

Gaisen (foreigner chasers). Men and women interested in Caucasians.

Garisen (skinny chasers). Gay men who like slim "twinks."

Hagesen (bald chasers). Gay men who like the rough, shaved-head look, but also women who have a thing for bald-headed men.

Higesen (beard chasers). Gay men who like men with facial hair.

Janiizusen (Johnnies chasers). Gay men who like handsome youths of the boy-band kind that are managed by Johnny Kitagawa's popular talent company, Johnny & Associates. Also *Janisen.*

Kanesen. Money chasers.

Kaosen (face chasers). Men and women who like a specific type of face, but do not have a preference for a particular physique (*taikaku*).

Karesen (withered chasers). Generally young women attracted to men who are beyond middle age.

Kegaresen (unclean chasers). Those preferring dirtier, unwashed partners. In gay circles it mainly refers to men who like the blue-collar and autoworker types in dirty overalls.

Kumasen (bear chasers). Gay men who like large, hairy men.

Mamesen (bean chaser). In gay slang, men who like shorter men. Also known as *chibisen* (midget chaser).

Mikesen (three-digit chasers). Men and women into very heavy partners, weighing three digits and beyond; in other words, over 100kg (210 lb).

Nyūhāfusen (new-half chasers). Men interested in transsexuals, or *misuta rēdizu* (Mr. Ladies), transvestites.

Nonkesen (nongay chasers). Gay men who prefer sexual activity with straight men.

Okesen. A contraction of *kanoke* (coffin) and *sen* (chasers). For those who prefer extremely old partners.

Oyajisen (dad chasers). Men and women who prefer men old enough to be their fathers.
Potchasen (plump chasers). Also *potchirisen*.
Rimansen (short for "salary man" chasers). Men and women attracted to white-collar workers.
Shotasen (*shota* chasers). Men interested in underage boys. *Shota* is short for *Shōtarō konpurekkusu*, a colloquial Japanese term for pedophilia.
Sūtsusen (suit chasers). Men and women who are attracted to men in suits, or well-to do businessmen who will also wine and dine them.
Wakasen. Young chasers.
Yuruposen (wobble-plump chasers). Men interested in out-of-shape, beer-bellied type men.

(SENZURI. Masturbation.)

The most common word for male masturbation in Japanese is *senzuri*, literally "a thousand rubs." (Female masturbation is *manzuri*, "ten thousand rubs.") It is essentially a slang expression analogous to the English "jerking off." Its long standing popularity, however—it has been used since the Edo period (1603–1868)—has given it semiofficial standing, as indicated by its appearance in some of the more progressive dictionaries. It can be used with the verbs *suru, yaru, kaku*, and *koku*, all meaning "to do" or "to perform."

Ore daitai ichinichi ni ikkai senzuri yaru yo.
I usually jerk off like once a day.
Atashi mada otoko ga senzuri suru no dō yaru ka wakannai.
I still don't get how guys jerk off.
Atchi itte! Jibun de senzuri kokina!
Get away from me! Just go jerk off on your own!

Following the time-honored Japanese slang tradition of inverting words in order to make them incomprehensible to the casual bystander, *senzuri* was also reversed. The resulting *zurisen* has a rough, street-smart ring to it.

> *Ore mukashi, ie no ura de zurisen koite'ta toki mitsu-katchimatta koto aru'n da.*
> I was caught once beating off behind the house.
> *Omē konna zasshi de zurisen yatte'ru nante yūn ja nē yo! Kimochi warui!*
> Don't tell me you beat off looking at those magazines! Gross!
> *Ore gei-sauna ni haitte itta toki asetta ze! Oyaji minna zurisen koite yagatta!*
> I had a total shock when I walked into that gay sauna! All these old guys were beating off!

Two official foreign words that are commonly used are *masutabēshon*, from the English word "masturbation," and *onanii*, from the German word *Onanie*, which was introduced by German doctors during the 1870s. Unlike *senzuri*, which is used only for male masturbation, *masutabēshon* and *onanii* are both unisex. Over the years the clinical *onanii* has acquired a slightly coarse aura that has made it a favorite in sex-trade talk and pornography.

> *Ano pātii no ato, ore sugē kōfun shichatte, nikai mo masutabēshon shichatta!*
> I was so horny after that party, I jacked off twice!
> *Omē, masutabēshon yarinagara ketsu no ana ni baibu tsukkomuno'tte ii ze.*
> You should try sticking a dildo up your ass while you're whacking off—it's great.
> *Ore aniki ga heya de onanii shite'ru toko mitsukechatta.*
> I caught my brother jerking off in his room.

> **Tondemonē yo! Otoko minna koko no shawa de onanii shitenno!**
> This is fucking disgusting! All the guys whack off in this shower!

The noun *onanii* even has its own verb now, *onaru*.

> **Aitsu heya de hitori de terebi minagara onatta yo.**
> He was alone in his room watching TV and jerking off.

Onanii also appears in various interesting combinations:

Baibu onanii. Vibrator masturbation.
Kaikyaku-onanii (open-legged masturbation). Masturbation in a lying position, with legs spread apart.
Kappumen-onanii (cup-ramen masturbation). A trend in which instant ramen noodles and their plastic cup are used as a masturbatory aid.
Kawa-onanii (skin masturbation). A male masturbatory technique in which only the foreskin is pulled or rubbed.
Kitō-onanii (glans masturbation). A method of male masturbation in which only the head of the penis is rubbed.
Ona-Niito (masturbatory NEET). An unemployed loner who spends much of his or her time masturbating in front of the computer.*
Onachatto (masturbatory chat). Online chatting that involves masturbation.
Onachū. A contraction of *onanii* and *chūdokusha,* "addict."
Onahōru. A contraction of *onanii* and "hole." A masturbatory aid known in America as a "pocket pussy." Also *onaho,* for short. Other names for pocket pussy are *onaheru,* "masturbation helper," and *rabuhōru,* which is either from

---

*The British official acronym NEET, which stands for "Not in Employment, Education, or Training," has become a popular Japanese trend-word for a new class of the chronically unemployed (and unemployable).

the English "love hole" or "rub hole." Electric models are called *dendō-onahōru*, "electric pocket-pussy."

Onakappu (masturbatory cup). A device that looks like a tin can (and is sometimes disguised as one) into which the penis can be inserted to simulate sex. Devices that look like flashlights are called by their English-derived name *fureshuraito*, mistaken by many Japanese to mean "fresh light" (as in the popular hair-coloring brand), but which in fact is the punning "fleshlight."

Onakurabu. Short for *onaniikurabu*. A "masturbation club" in which masturbating customers can watch scantily clothed or semi-nude models. In some *onakurabu*, the hostesses or hosts will also perform *tekoki*, "hand jobs."

Onanii-tō (masturbation faction). A sex-trade term for men who prefer masturbation or masturbatory games to sexual intercourse.

Onaniigudzu. Masturbatory goods or aids.

Onaniikanshō (masturbation appreciation). A sex-club service in which customers can "appreciate" or watch a *kompanyon* (hostess) masturbate.

Onapetto (masturbatory pet). A favorite porn actor or actress watched during masturbation. Also known as *onafure*, "masturbation friend."

Panonanii (underwear or panty masturbation). A variety of male or female masturbation techniques in which the underwear is not removed. *Panonaniifechi*, "underwear masturbation fetish," refers to individuals who either like watching or performing this form of masturbation.

Sōgo onanii. Mutual masturbation.

Yagai onanii. "Outdoors masturbation" (in public areas), also known as *aokan onanii*, literally "green mischief masturbation."

The word *masutabēshon* might not be as popular as *onanii*, but *masu* (the first two syllables of "masturbation") is. It appears as a verb in the form *masu o kaku*, "stroking a *masu*." *Masu* is also often lengthened into *masutabē*. A funny little pun on *masu* used in Kobe City is *Suma no ura*, "Suma backward": the two syllables of *Suma* (a district in the western part of the city) read "backward" are *masu*.

Another interesting *masu* neologism is *masukatto*, a pun on "mascot," "muscat," and *masu katto*, "masturbation cut." This is said when one cannot find opportunities to masturbate.

> ***Ore biichi ni iku to dōmo masu o kakitaku natchimaun da yo na.***
> Whenever I'm at the beach I get this urge to whack off.
> ***Ore kanojo to neru'n dattara masu o kaiteta hō ga ii ya!***
> I'd rather beat off than sleep with her!
> ***Aitsu ga kangaete'ru koto wa itsumo suma no ura dake da yo.***
> All he thinks about is jerking off.

One of the native Japanese words for male masturbation is the melodious *shiko shiko*, "rub rub," which also exists as the verb *shikoru*, which in standard Japanese means "to stiffen." A related word is *poshiko*, a contraction of *chimpo* (penis) and *shiko* (rub).

> ***Nē shiko shiko suru no'tte hada ni iin da'tte honto ka yo?***
> You think it's true that jerking off's good for the skin?
> ***Otoko'tte jibun de shikoru no shinai furi surun da mon! Hen da yo ne!***
> Isn't it weird how guys always act like they never jerk off?

General terms for masturbation that can be used by both sexes are the more euphemistic *jibun de yaru*, "doing it on one's own"; *hitoride de yaru*, "doing it by oneself"; *hitorigokko*, "self-play"; and *hitori-echi*, "self-sex."

> ***Ammari jibun de yaru no'tte abunē ka na?***
> I wonder if it's bad for you to play with yourself too much?

> *Atashi hajimete hitori de yatta no wa, jūhachi no toki datta to omou!*
> The first time I played with myself was when I was eighteen!
> *Shinjirareru ka? Kagami o minagara hitori-echi surun da ze!*
> Do you believe this? He looks at himself in a mirror while he's playing with it!

Other general words for masturbation, used throughout Japan by all age groups, are *shigoki* and its verb form *shigoku*, "to stroke" or "squeeze a thing through one's hand."

> *Asoko o shigoku.*
> He's playing with his thing.
> *Aitsu hen na yatsu da yo! Kondōmu kabusete shigoki su'n da'tte yo.*
> That dude's weird! He wears a condom to jerk off.
> *Ore shigoku no'tte ii to omou yo!*
> I kinda like jerking off!

When an individual displays eccentricity in his or her masturbatory patterns, such as doing it in public, the action would be classified in street slang as *hen suru*, "doing the weird." A contraction of *hen* (weird) and the staple term *senzuri* (a thousand rubs) has also created *henzuri*.

> *Hitomae de hen shita koto aru?*
> Did you ever play with yourself in front of anyone?
> *Kinō sā, densha no naka de tonari no otoko ga hen shiten no yo.*
> The guy next to me in the subway, like, was beating his meat.

Some of the rougher words for masturbation come from the sex trade. *Yubiman*, "finger cunt," is either a man forming his hand into the shape of a vagina and masturbating on his own, or a woman using her hand on a man in lieu of her vagina. "Soapland" and "Health" massage parlors as well as other sex establishments offer what is known as *fingā sābisu*, "finger service"; *fingā purē*, "finger play"; and *fashon massāji*, "fashion massage," as part of their roster of masturbatory services.

(SHŌBEN. Urine.)

The technical term for urine, *nyō*, is not used in everyday speech unless the speaker is talking about medical subjects like urine tests (*nyō kensa*). The Japanese word that best parallels the English "urine" in nuance and texture is the traditional euphemism *shōben*, "small convenience" (its opposite, *daiben*, "large convenience," is the euphemism of choice for feces). In everyday speech, however, *shōben* is superseded by its slangier variation *shomben*, which has the colloquial edge of English words like "piss" or "taking a leak."

While the maturer man, even in informal speech, might still opt for the conventional *shōben*, the younger crowd usually uses *shomben*.

> *Omē! Tanomu kara! Michi de shōben shinai de kure yo na!*
> C'mon now! Please don't urinate in the street!
> *Chotto shomben itte kuru wa!*
> I'm just going for a quick leak!

A variation on *shomben* is *tachishomben*, "standing piss," and its shortened version *tachishon*.

> *Otoko wa minna ano kado de tachishomben shite'ru!*
> The guys are all in that corner taking a leak!

> **Anta, koko Tōkyō nan dakara! Daremo tachishomben suru hito nanka nai wa yo!**
> C'mon honey! This is Tokyo! People don't just piss in the street.

Another *shōben* word is *tsureshōben*, "pissing together." It started off as a village expression, used when people would take a break in their fieldwork to go off together for a piss. Today people still quote the proverb *Inaka no tsureshōben*, "Pissing together in the country." Unlike townspeople, Japanese villagers are very relaxed in matters concerning the body and its functions.

Nowadays *tsureshōben* is a sign of friendship, and has become especially popular in schools and offices, where young women often go off to the toilet in droves for a "wee-wee" and a chat. Teachers who watch their classes systematically empty out as the result of a severe case of *tsureshōben* might gruffly shout:

> **Tsureshōben yamenasai!**
> This going off for a piss together must stop!
> **Zen'in issho ni tsureshōben ikanaide hoshii!**
> Please don't all go at the same time!

Another *tsureshōben* proverb worth memorizing is *Tsureshōben, tabi ni michi*, "Pissing together on the road." This proverb indicates that urinating together during an outing or a picnic is a sign of friendship. Ideally, close friends should be able to drop formalities.

When it comes to urine, there are words chiefly used by men (*shomben, tsureshomben*) and words predominantly used by women. Even though the technical term for urine, *nyō*, is not used in colloquial speech, it has played an important role by supplying Japanese slang with its urine-related vocabulary for women. The character for *nyō* (made up of the ideograms "tail" and "water") can also be read as *shito*, which developed into the dialect words *oshikko* and *shishi* (predominantly in the Harima region.)* These words, being softer than *shomben*, have been taken up in everyday speech and are today the slang words for peeing that are preferred by women. (Men might use *oshikko* when speaking to women, but would consider it effeminate to use among themselves.)

> **Chotto matte'te! Umi ni haitte oshikko shite kuru kara!**
> Wait a minute! I'm going into the water to take a whiz!
> **Aa, mō, ki ni shinai! Mō kono kōen de shishi shichaē!**
> Oh, I don't care anymore! I'm gonna pee right here in the park!

Some provincial variations on *shomben* and *oshikko* that sound comical in Tokyo, and are thus used in jest, are *shombe*, from the Harima dialect; *shiko*, from the Jinji and the Kawachi-gun dialects; and *shiiko*, from the Tochigi dialect.

> **Chotto shitsurei! Ore shombe itte kimasu!**
> Would you please excuse me, I've got to go for a piss!
> **Wakai onna no ko wa soto de shiko nanka shimasen yo!**
> A young girl shouldn't piss outside!
> **Aa! 'Ya da! Kono ko mata pantsu ni shiiko shichatte!**
> Oh, no! The little brat pissed his pants again!

Nyō and *shito* have been used in colloquial speech since pre-medieval times. Two memorable *shito* haiku are Yamazaki Sokan's (1464–1552) mildly blasphemous:

Saohime no	The goddess of spring
Harutachinagara	Standing
Shito o shite	Takes a piss

And Matsuo Basho's (1664–94) earthy description of his stay in a desolate mountain hut:

Nomi shirami	Fleas, lice
Uma no shito suru	And a horse pissing
Makura moto	By my pillow

A comic reference to a man's urinating is *tsutsuharai.* *Tsutsu,* "pipe," is a slang word for penis, and *harai* means "to shake off." Thus *tsutsuharai* can also mean "to shake the penis after urinating."

> *Ore minna no mae de nanka, tsutsuharai dekinē!*
> I can't just piss in front of everyone!
> *Chanto tsutsuharai suru no wasurenaide yo!*
> Don't forget to shake off your thing after pissing!

One of the specialties of hard-core Japanese street slang is its collection of expressions dedicated to women urinating. Most of these terms capitalize on words suggestive of loud showerlike gushes. Two expressions that use natural phenomena to bring their point home are *gōu,* "downpour," and *yūdachi,* "sudden shower."

> *Aitsu-ra futari de issho ni gōu shi ni ita yo.*
> The two of them went to pop a squat.
> *Ano onna no yūdachi no oto ga sugokute, bā kauntā made kikoeta yo!*
> The sound of her pissing was so loud, you could hear it all the way to the bar.

Two other sex-trade expressions for a woman's urinating are *teppō mizu,* "flash flood," and *manshon.* To the uninitiated Japanese ear, *manshon* means "apartment." This slang expression did not originate from the English "mansion," but from combining *man,* "cunt," and *shon* (short for *shomben*), "piss."

> *Hanashi kakenaide yo! Ima teppō mizu no saichū nan dakara!*
> Don't talk to me now! I'm pissing like a race horse!
> *Chotto koko de matte'te! Atashi manshon shite kuru kara!*
> Wait for me here! I'm going to pop a squat!

(SURI. Pickpocket.)

Suri, the standard Japanese expression for pickpocket, was inspired by *suritsukeru,* "rubbing against," which is what your run-of-the-mill pickpocket does in buses, train stations, and especially the overcrowded rush-hour subways. To get pickpocketed in Japanese is expressed idiomatically as *suri ni au,* "encountering a pickpocket."

> *Kyō suri ni atte, tokei o torareta.*
> Some pickpocket swiped my watch today.
> *Chikatetsu ni nottara ki o tsukero yo! Suri darake dakara na!*
> Careful riding on the subway! It's fulla pickpockets!

The pickpockets are a strong and, by Western standards, well-organized group on the Japanese streets. They speak their own jargon, often unintelligible to outsiders, and have contributed a sizable vocabulary to mainstream criminal street slang, the "hidden language," *ingo.* One of the common insider terms on the streets for the pickpocket, inspired by his typical trait of constantly being on the lookout, is *ai-chan,* "Little Mr. Coincidence."

> *Onegai dakara, anna ai-chan renchū to tsukiau no wa yoshite yo!*
> I wish you wouldn't keep hanging out with that bunch of jostlers!
> *Aitsu ai-chan datta kedo ima ja yaku ni te dashite'ru.*
> He used to be a pickpocket, now he's dealing in drugs.

Another favorite term for pickpocket in the darker alleys of Tokyo is the provincial word *chibo.* Although it is not considered standard Japanese, its popularity in major dialects such as Kyoto, Osaka, Shikoku, Hiroshima, and Hokuriku has helped it gain a strong foothold on streets throughout Japan.

> *Nan da kono chibo! Ore no saifu ni te o dashiyagatte!*
> Man! That frisker laid his hands on my wallet!
> *Chibo yatte'ru no'tte omoshirē ze!*
> Being a frisker's fun!

Some of the "friskers" or "fingersmiths," as they are known on the American streets, are women. The Japanese lady pickpocket is known in street circles as *posuto*, "mailbox": anything she swipes gets stuffed down her blouse, like a letter into a mailbox.

> *Ano onna posuto datta! Ore no mono zembu totte nigeyagatta!*
> That woman was a pickpocket! She took all my stuff!
> *Ano posuto wa kao mo sugē kirei datta shi, teguchi mo kōmyō datta ze.*
> That girl pickpocket's not only good-looking, she works well too.

Belonging to the same group of pickpockets is the *wappa hazushi,* who specializes in snatching rings and bracelets off his victim's hands. This *ingo* criminal-slang term is made up of *wappa,* "ring" or "bracelet," and *hazusu,* "to unfasten."

> *Ano wappa hazushi honto ni kurōto da ze! Aitsu no shigoto mita koto aru kai?*
> That ring thief's a real pro! Have you seen him work?
> *Aitsu-ra wappa hazushi tsukamaeyō to shita'n dakedo, nigerarechimatta.*
> They tried catching that ring swiper, but he got away.

A related type of street criminal is the *oihagi,* from *oi,* "to follow," and *hagi,* "stripping off." The *oihagi* started his career in old Japan as a highwayman, following, catching, and stripping hapless travelers of their belongings. On today's Japanese streets, he has been transmogrified into a purse snatcher.

> *Oihagi ga ushiro kara kite, atashi no baggu hittakutte ita.*
> That purse snatcher came up behind me and grabbed my bag.
> *Zettai ni atashi no mono totte itta oihagi mitsukerare-nai to omou na!*
> I'm sure they'll never find that purse snatcher who took all my things!

The victim or "target" of any of the above thieves is known in *ingo* slang as *gaisha*, short for *higaisha*, "victim," or rather sardonically as *kyaku*, "customer."

> *Kyō wa nannin no gaisha ni atatta'n dai?*
> How many scores didja do today?
> *Ichiban ii kyaku'tte no wa, chikatetsu no naka no yatsu darō na.*
> The best easy marks, I guess, are the ones in the subway.

When pickpocket specialists convene for in-depth conversation, outsiders, even if they are criminals of a different persuasion, find it difficult to fathom what is being said. Every method and hand movement involved in pickpocketing has a specialized terminology, not to mention the insider words for all the objects stolen.

Thus *uguisu*, a small songbird favored in traditional Japanese poetry, takes on the meaning of "gold watch." The word "ring," known in standard Japanese as *yubiwa*, "finger ring," is inverted in pickpocket slang, resulting in *wayubi*, or transformed into *waibi*, or *guruwa*, "round-ring." The wallet is known as *iwa*, or "rock," and the empty wallet is *iwagara*, "rock-empty"; if an individual takes the money and then throws the wallet away, the term of choice would be *iwagaracharu*, "rock-emptying."

Some of the key Japanese pickpocket words are the names of the different pockets where the coveted wallet might be. The back pocket, or "ass pocket," is known as *shiriba*, "ass place"; an outside pocket is known as *sotoba*, "outside place"; and the harder-to-get-at inside pocket is the *uchiba*, "inside place."

> ***Ano otoko iwa o shiriba ni ireteta kara raku datta ze.***
> That guy had his wallet in his back pocket, so it was a pushover.
> ***Ichiban yariyasui gaisha wa yappa' sotoba ni kane irete'ru toshiyori da yo na!***
> The easiest targets are those old idiots who carry their money in their outside pockets!
> ***Ore ga ima neratta yatsu, uchiba datta kara yariniku-katta ze!***
> The guy I just did was tough! It was in his inside pocket!

(UNKO. Shit.)

To translate the exact nuance of *unko* into English, one would need an expression midway between an earthy "shit" and a more playful "poot." It is this dichotomy of the vulgar and the cute that makes *unko* Japan's favorite expression for chatting casually about feces.

Unko's etymology is much disputed among Japanologists. One theory is that *un* is an imitation of the deep-throated grunt sometimes discharged during an arduous bout of defecation, while *ko,* the diminutive suffix, gives the word its euphemistic texture. A more formalistic school of thought asserts that this expression was inspired by the Japanese hiragana syllabary: the first syllable, *a,* symbolizing food entering the mouth, and the last syllable, *un,* representing food departing from the anus. Although *unko* is a slang word, its universal popularity endears it to respectable grannies as much as to the not-so-respectable criminal elements.

> ***Ken wa toire de unko shite'ru no.***
> Ken's taking a shit in the toilet.
> ***Chotto unko ga shitai kara, koko de matte'te!***
> Wait for me here, I have to go for a quick shit!

To give *unko* an extra slangy "oomph," speakers sometimes opt for the juicier *bakuon unko,* "explosive shit."

> *Aa! Yatto ma ni atta ze! Nante bakuon unko darō!*
> Man, I made it just in time! That was quite a dump I took there!
> *Ano ko resutoran de sugē bakuon unko suru kara, minna taberu no yametchatta janai yo!*
> At the restaurant she took such a loud shit everyone like stopped eating!

One version of *unko* that is thought to be more *kawaii,* "cute," is *unchi,* whose childlike playfulness makes it a favorite among the girls.

> *Aa! Gomen! Atashi unchi shita kara ima hairu to kusai yo!*
> Whoops! Don't go in there now! I just took a shit, so it stinks!
> *'Ya da atashi! Konna soto de unchi dekinai wa yo!*
> No way! I can't just take a shit out here!

A nasty new slang word for "squat," inspired by *unchi,* is *unchingu sutairu,* "shitting style," an Anglo-Japanese expression that was created by adding *-ingu* (as in shitt-*ing*) to *unchi,* "shit," and then sticking on *sutairu,* the English word "style." An even rougher version, *unkozuwari,* "shit sitting," is favored by the younger street-crowd.

> *Sonna unchingu sutairu de suwaranaide!*
> Don't squat as if you were taking a shit!
> *Nan de aitsu-ra unkozuwari de basu matte yagaru? Koko inaka ja nai yo!*
> Why are these guys squatting in such a disgusting way at that bus stop? It's not like we're in some field!

A playful variation on *unko* is the dialect word *onkobo,* a term originally from the Chōzu dialect. It is considered side-splittingly funny in Tokyo, where the in crowd is constantly on the prowl for the most *dasai* (uncool) sounding provincial words. These words are picked up and used as facetiously as possible, often followed by raucous peals of laughter, at the expense of those less elegant in speech.

> **Dare ga niwa ni onkobo shita no ka ne?**
> All right! Who dropped a turd in the garden?
> **Aa warui kedo, onkobo ni ikitai!**
> Sorry, but I have to drop a log!

The other key slang word for "shit" in Japanese is *kuso.* The character for *kuso* is made up of two components: "tail" on top, and "rice" on the bottom, and is closely related to the character for *nyo,* "urine," which is made up of "tail" on top, and "water" on the bottom. *Kuso* is as widely used as *unchi,* but has a slightly rougher quality. It is similar to the English "shit" in that besides its literal reference to feces, it is also used as an expletive indicating rage or frustration. *Kuso!* can be translated as "Shit!" "Damn!" or "Fuck!" It can also be used as an emphatic prefix: *kuso-baba,* "fuckin' bitch," or *kuso-kuruma,* "fuckin' car."

> **Toire wa doko da? Ore kuso ga shitē!**
> Where's the toilet? I have to go for a crap!
> **Onegai dakara! Kuso shita ato nagasu no wasurenaide kure yo!**
> Please! I wish you wouldn't forget to flush after you take a shit!

When defecation takes place out in the open, like in a garden, park, or on the sidewalk, a popular slang term is *no-guso,* "field shit," which was originally used in the strict sense of defecating out in the fields, away from one's hut. Nowadays, due to widespread urbanization, *noguso* has become more ductile in meaning.

> **Anta noguso shinaide yo! Koko Tokyo dakara! Saitama ja nai yo!**
> I wish you wouldn't shit outside! This is Tokyo, not Saitama!*
> **Minna ga mite'ru no ni noguso nanka dekinai yo!**
> I can't take a shit out here with everyone watching!

A punny street-slang variant on *kuso* is *kyū-jū*, "nine-ten." The link between these numerals and feces is that the characters for "nine" and "ten," usually read *kyū* and *jū*, can also be read as *ku* and *so*. In the rare case that this variant is actually put in writing, like on the wall of a public toilet, it will appear either in the characters for "nine" and "ten," or—the ultimate in radicality—the numerals "9/10."

> **Kuruma tomete kurenai? Chotto kyūjū ga shitai'n da yo ne!**
> Can you stop the car? I just wanna drop a quick turd!
> **Babā ga kyūjū shita ato'tte doko mo kashiko mo kusakute tamannē!**
> When the old woman takes a crap the whole place stinks sky-high!

A colorful but somewhat coarse synonym for defecating, popular among the younger generation, is *mori mori suru*. The term *mori mori* is in itself a harmless adverb suggesting intense activity, such as *mori mori kū,* "to eat like crazy," or *mori mori benkyō suru,* "to study like crazy." But the reason teenagers saw

---

*Saitama, which is right outside Tokyo, has been traditionally used by Tokyoites as the ultimate symbol of provinciality.

mori mori as a prime candidate for a feisty analogy for shit is that when used alone, it evokes a sense of rapid piling up.

> **Uchi no otōto ima mori mori shite'ru kara, haitcha dame yo!**
> My brother's dumping in there, don't go in!
> **Chotto kami chōdai! Atashi mori mori ni ikitai no yo.**
> Give me some paper! I have to take a dump.

When one specifically wishes to discuss a piece of shit, as opposed to the act of defecating itself, street-slang terms used by the young would be *toguro,* "coil," and more general expressions like *ōkii no,* a "big one," or *ōkii yatsu,* a "large guy."

> **Mō toire ni sugoi toguro ga atta yo! Dare ga yatta no?**
> There's a big turd in the toilet! Who did it?
> **Obā-chan! Ōkii no ga deta yo!**
> Grandma! I did a big one!
> **Komatta na! Toire ga nai nante! Ore ōkii yatsu shite'n da yo!**
> Damn! There's no toilet around here! I've gotta dump a load!

(WANPATAN. Boring.)

Wanpatan (with the stress on the first and last *a*) belongs to the growing body of "made in Japan" English expressions. These fashionable words are known as *waseigo*, "Japan-made language," and they are created when Western words or phrases, usually English, are modified, redefined, and then absorbed into everyday speech.*

Wanpatan is the Japanese pronunciation of "one pattern," which from a logical standpoint is the perfect synonym for "boring." In modern Japanese, parties, people, books, food, or anything at all can be labeled *wanpatan*.

> *Kare-ra no pātii wa itsumo wanpatan da yo! Zurakare!*
> Their parties are always so boring! Let's split!
> *Kare'tte itsumo wanpatan na gyagu shika iwanai'n da mon! Saitei!*
> His jokes are *so* stale! The worst!

In Tokyo school yards, witty youngsters have engendered the zaniest analogies for the word "boring" that the Japanese language can boast. The basis of these clever neologisms is the

---

Waseigo words range from ordinary expressions like *poketto beru*, "pocket bell," for beeper; and *uerunessu dorinku*, "wellness drink," for sports shake; to more risqué terms like *daburu purē*, "double play," for fellatio; or *sukuryū*, "screw," for penis.

semantic reinterpretation of *wanpatan,* which these creative youngsters dissolved into *wan,* "woof," as in "bark," and *patan,* "bang." The resulting expression is the hilarious *koketa inu,* the "stumbling dog." (When the poor animal stumbles, one is likely to hear a woof followed by a bang).

> *Kyō no miitingu mata koketa inu!*
> Today's meeting was so *boring*!
> *Eikaiwa no kurasu ikitaku nai wa! Dōse koketa inu nan dakara!*
> I don't wanna go to my English class! It's such a drag!

Another droll synonym for "boring" that sprang from the "woof-bang" school is *inu no soto,* the "dog outside," the concept here being that the dog went "woof," the door went "bang," and—*Wan!! Patan!!*—the dog was shut out.

> *Atashi yoku ano disuko ni itte'ta kedō, ima mō inu no soto da mon nē!*
> I used to go to that club all the time, but it's gotten like totally dull!
> *Aitsu jibun de wa omoshiroi to omotte'n da ze! Tada no inu no soto no kuse shite yo!*
> He thinks he's so cool, but he's such a major yawn!

(YARU. To do in.)

Yaru, literally "to do," is one of the older and more vicious Japanese underworld expressions for killing. It has been a long-time criminal expression in Japan which, like its American equivalent "doing someone in," has become a favorite since it was taken up by the Yakuza movies of 1950s and '60s.

> *Aitsu o yare!*
> Let's do him in!
> *Aitsu o yatta!*
> I bumped him off!

The standard Japanese word for killing or murdering is *korosu.* It is a powerful and negative word; its character, which can also be read as *satsu,* appears in many lethal terms: *koroshi,* "killing"; *koroshiya,* "hired killer"; *satsu batsu to shita,* "brutal"; *satsugai,* "slaying"; *satsujin,* "homicide"; *satsujin hannin,* "murderer"; *jisatsu,* "suicide"; and *satsuriku,* "massacre." This scary character is made up of the two elements "pig" and "smite," the idea being the killing of a pig. By the time the term was shipped to Japan, its meaning had already shifted to imply killing in general. For a fiercer and slangier edge, the prefix *bu-* is added, resulting in *bukkorosu,* "totally kill." *Korosu* and *bukkorosu* can also be used idiomatically to mean "beating the shit out of."

> *Omē kane harawanē nara, korosu ze!*
> I'll kill you if you don't hand over the cash!
> *Aitsu, satsu ni tarekondari shitara bukkoroshite yaru!*
> If he squeals to the cops we'll fuckin' kill him!

Beyond the familiar expressions *yaru* and *korosu*, there exists a whole roster of street words involving killing and death that are still cherished among the criminal *ingo* (hidden language) speakers, but have never been launched by the media into mainstream speech. One of these is *mageru*, "to twist" or "to bend."

> *Dare ga ano jiji mageta'n da yo? Omē-ra?*
> Who killed that old dude? Was it you guys?
> *Ore-tachi hikkoshita ze! Magerarechimau mon na!*
> We moved outta there! We were gonna get killed!

Another old-timer on the *ingo* slang-scene is *shimeru*, literally "to close."

> *Ano baba aitsu-ra ni shimerareta ze! Shirisugite'ta kara na!*
> They finished that bitch off! She knew too much!
> *Ano renchū ittai nannin shimeta'n da? Kono futari dake?*
> How many guys did that group wipe out? Only those two?

On the same *ingo* slang-word list is *tomeru*, "to stop."

> *Kotoshi no rokugatsu, aitsu-ra uchi no jiji o tometa!*
> Last June they bumped off my old man!
> *Ano yarō ki ni sawaru'n dattara, tometchimae yo!*
> If he gets in the way, kill him!

Another rough criminal slang-term used to chat about killing people is *tatamu*, "to fold."

> *Aitsu-ra ano otoko o tatande kawa ni nagesuteta!*
> They finished him off and threw him in the river!
> *Aitsu tatanjimaō ze! Kane wa yamawake da!*
> Let's finish him off and split the cash!

A vicious euphemism for murder popular among the criminal crowd is *nesaseru,* "to put to sleep."

> *Aitsu nesaseta ato, karada wa dō surun no yo?*
> What am I supposed to do with his body after I've finished him off?
> *Ano renchū ima keimusho ni haitte'ru! Nannin ka nesasechimatta kara na!*
> That bunch is in prison now! Who knows how many people they've bumped off!

In the same group of hard-line street-words for murder is *chirasu,* "to scatter."

> *Dare ano chiraseta onna? Omae shitte'ru?*
> Who's that woman they got rid of?
> *Ore daremo chirasanē ze! Jodan ja nē yo!*
> No way, man! I'm not doing no killing!

(ZUKKYŪ!! Heart Attack!!)

Listen to young American street surfers with their wave boards talking about their newest skating tricks, and you might hear a string of sound words: "He did an ollie—*blam!*—and then a light board leap—*whack!*—and then a kickflip—*zurrk!*"

A new generation of young Japanese that has grown up with manga and anime uses a flood of cartoonish sound-words in almost every situation. Anime geeks—*anime otaku*, or *aniota* for short—often seem to be living in a cartoon bubble. Unlike American skaters, Japanese youngsters use sound words in surprisingly nuanced ways. The trend in Japan is to either express emotion with a sound word—*"Uki-uki!"* (girlish excitement), *"Uho!"* (surprise at a sexy sight)—or to anticipate or follow almost every action with a Japanese *"Zap!"* or *"Bang!"*

A possible scenario: A young man walking down the street bites into a candy bar, and finding it dry, says *"Keho-keho,"* cough cough." He is taken aback—*"Are-are"* (surprise)—tears off the paper wrapper, and notices that the candy bar has almonds in it—*"Zukkyū!!"* (shock / heart attack). He hates almonds—*"Mukká!"* (anger)—and, exclaiming *"Pói!"* (wham), throws the candy bar away.

Another possible scenario: A girl trying on her new *akuse* (accessories) looks into the mirror and says *"Niko-niko"* (smile), and smiles. She is not sure about the earrings—*"Uuún!"*

(uncertain musing)—she looks closer—*"Gan!"* (Darn!)—takes them off, says *"Ban!"* (the sound of placing something on a hard surface), and puts the earrings on her dresser. She realizes her skin is feeling dry, says *"Shittori!"* (the sound of moisture on skin) and proceeds to rub some moisturizer on her face. Then suddenly—*"Kyaá!"* (horror)—she notices a pimple. She realizes to her horror that she has a date tonight—*"Chiin!"* (funeral bell).

Other sound words used to anticipate actions:

> **Chira!** Said when flashing a body part, followed by *porrori* or *piron* when whatever one is flashing pops out.
> **Chudōn!** Explosion!
> **Doro doro.** Confusion, uncertainty.
> **Fumu-fumu** (I understand). Said while nodding.
> **Gufufu** (male chuckle). *Uhuhu*. Girlish giggle.
> **Jii.** Stare.
> **Jitō.** Menacing stare.
> **Kon-kon.** Knocking on the door, followed by *gajá*, the sound of the door opening, followed by *Jaaan!* "Ta-da!" or "Here I am!"
> **Patchiri.** "Click," usually said before pressing a camera button.
> **Pita.** Said when one suddenly stops in one's tracks.
> **Potchi.** Said before pressing an elevator button.
> **Suri-suri.** Said by girls before or while cuddling something, usually a plush toy.
> **Uki-uki.** Girlish excitement.

Japanese Word List

Index